Scale 1: 300 000
or 4.7 miles to 1 inch
(3 km to 1 cm)

1st edition April 2004

© Automobile Association Developments Limited 2004

This product includes mapping based upon data licensed from Ordnance Survey of Northern Ireland® by permission of the Chief Executive, acting on behalf of the Controller of Her Majesty's Stationery Office. © Crown copyright 2004 Permit No. 30202. This product includes RCDI by permission of Ordnance Survey of Northern Ireland on behalf of the Controller of Her Majesty's Stationery Office. © Crown copyright 2004

Republic of Ireland mapping based on Ordnance Survey Ireland. Permit No. 7776.
© Ordnance Survey Ireland and Government of Ireland.

Many place names in the main-map section of this atlas are given in English and Irish. The names shown are those approved by the Ordnance Survey of Northern Ireland and Ordnance Survey Ireland.

The AA would like to acknowledge the following bodies and agencies for information used in the creation of this atlas:
The Environment & Heritage Service, Heritage of Ireland, RSPB, Department of Agriculture & Rural Development, Coillte Teoranta, The National Trust, An Taisce, Roads Service and The National Roads Authority.

Published by AA Publishing (a trading name of Automobile Association Developments Limited, whose registered office is Millstream, Maidenhead Road, Windsor, Berkshire SL4 5GD, UK. Registered number 1878835).

Mapping produced by the Cartography Department of The Automobile Association (A01116).

ISBN 0 7495 3544 X

A CIP catalogue record for this book is available from The British Library.

Printed in Italy by Printer Trento srl, Trento.

The contents of this atlas are believed to be correct at the time of the latest revision. However, the publishers cannot be held responsible for loss occasioned to any person acting or refraining from action as a result of any material in this atlas, nor for any errors, omissions or changes in such material. This does not affect your statutory rights. The publishers would welcome information to correct any errors or omissions and to keep this atlas up to date. Please write to the Cartographic Editor, Publishing Division, The Automobile Association, Fanum House, Basing View, Basingstoke, Hampshire RG21 4EA, UK.

Atlas contents

Map pages

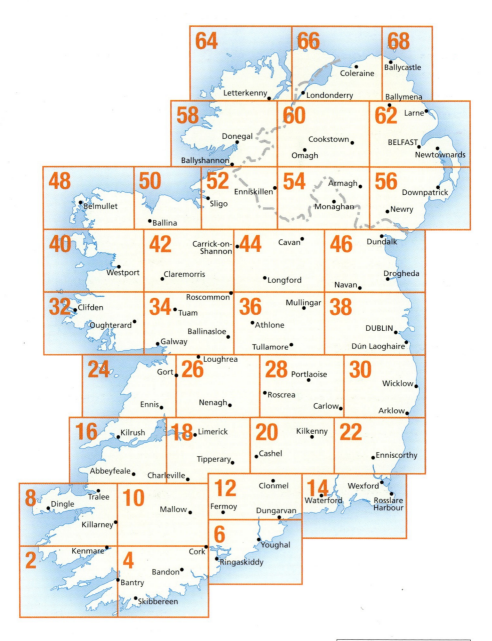

64

66

68

Ballycastle

Coleraine

Letterkenny · Londonderry · Ballymena

58 **60** **62** Larne ·

Donegal · Cookstown BELFAST ·

Omagh · Newtownards ·

Ballyshannon · · Armagh

48 **50** **52** **54** **56**

Belmullet · Enniskillen · Monaghan · Downpatrick

Sligo · Newry ·

Ballina ·

40 **42** Carrick-on- **44** Cavan · **46** Dundalk ·

Shannon

Westport · Claremorris · Longford · Drogheda ·

Navan · Roscommon

32 Clifden · **34** · Tuam **36** Mullingar · **38**

Oughterard · Ballinasloe Athlone · DUBLIN ·

Galway · Tullamore · Dún Laoghaire ·

Loughrea ·

24 **26** Gort · **28** Portlaoise · **30**

Roscrea · Wicklow ·

Ennis · Nenagh · Carlow · Arklow ·

16 Kilrush · **18** · Limerick **20** Kilkenny · **22**

Tipperary · Cashel · Enniscorthy ·

Abbeyfeale · Charleville ·

8 Tralee · **10** **12** Clonmel · **14** Wexford ·

Dingle · Mallow · Fermoy · Waterford · Rosslare
Dungarvan · Harbour

Killarney ·

2 Kenmare · **4** Cork · **6** Youghal

Bandon · Ringaskiddy ·

Bantry ·

Skibbereen ·

0	10	20	30	40	50 miles
0	20	40	60	80 km	

Key to map symbols

Motoring information

M1	Toll-free motorway
M1 Toll	Toll motorway
	Full, restricted junction
	Motorway under construction
	Dual carriageway
	Single carriageway
	Road under construction
	Minor road
Toll	Bridge or road toll
	Car ferry
	Catamaran car ferry
	Railway, station, level crossing
	Airport, airfield
	City, town, village or locality
628	Height in metres, pass

CORK	Primary destination (selected)
N17	National primary route (IRL)
N56	National secondary route (IRL)
R182	Regional road (IRL)
8	Distance in kilometres (IRL)
A4	Primary route (NI)
A21	A road (NI)
B75	B road (NI)
5	Distance in miles (NI)
)=========(	Road tunnel
	International boundary
	Other boundary
	Beach, other foreshore
	River, canal, lough
31	Page continuation number

Touring information

	Tourist information
	Tourist information (seasonal)
	Visitor centre
	AA approved campsite
	Other caravan site
	Abbey, cathedral or priory
	Ruined abbey, cathedral or priory
	Castle, hill-fort
	Museum or gallery
	Garden, country park
	Zoo, wildlife or bird park
	Nature, bird reserve
	Waymarked walk
	Viewpoint, picnic site
	AA listed, other golf course

	Scenic route
	Horse racing, motor-racing circuit
	International athletics, rugby union
	Boating, skiing activities
NT AT	National Trust property
	Historic house or building
	National Park
	Forest Park
	Woodland
	Prehistoric monument
	Industrial interest
1531	Battle site with date
	Monument, other place of interest
	Boxed symbols indicate attractions within urban areas

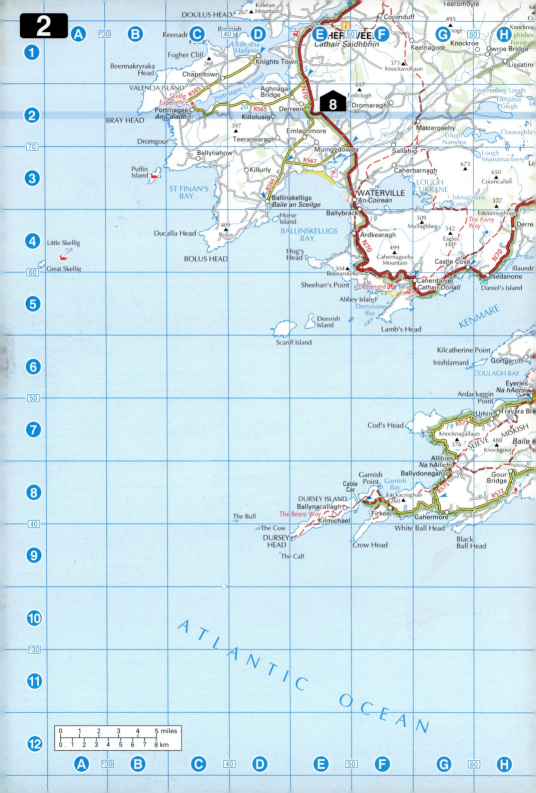

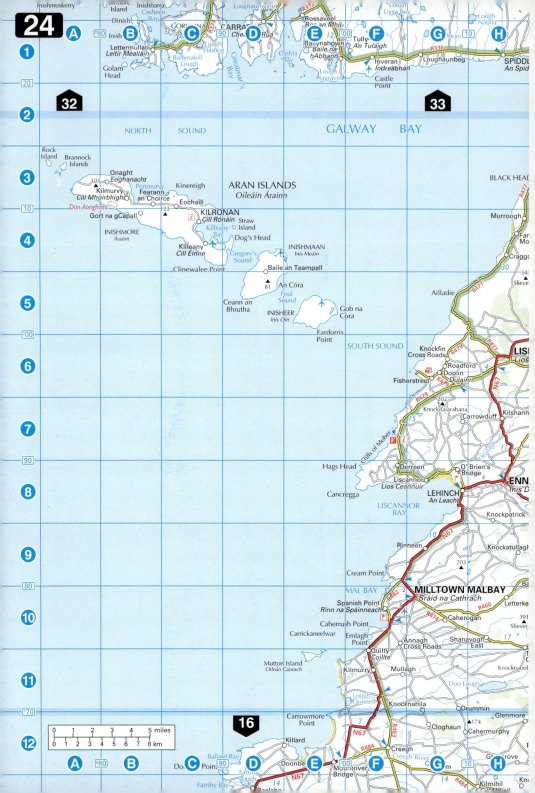

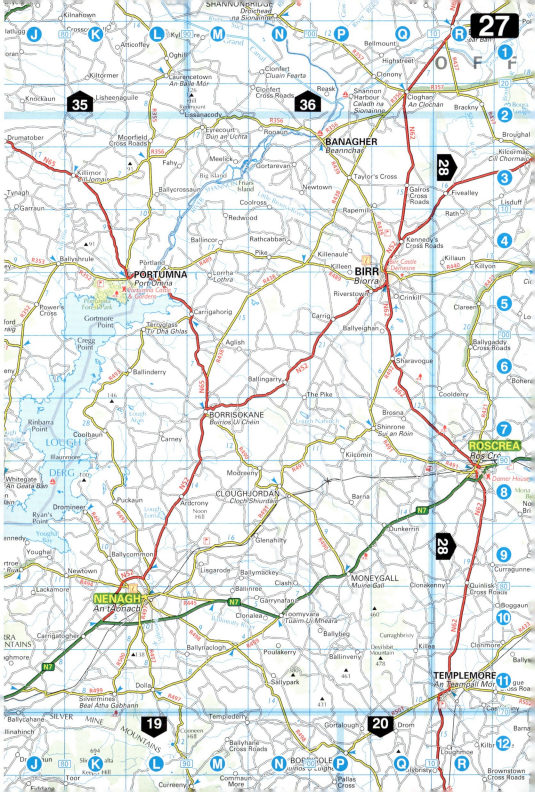

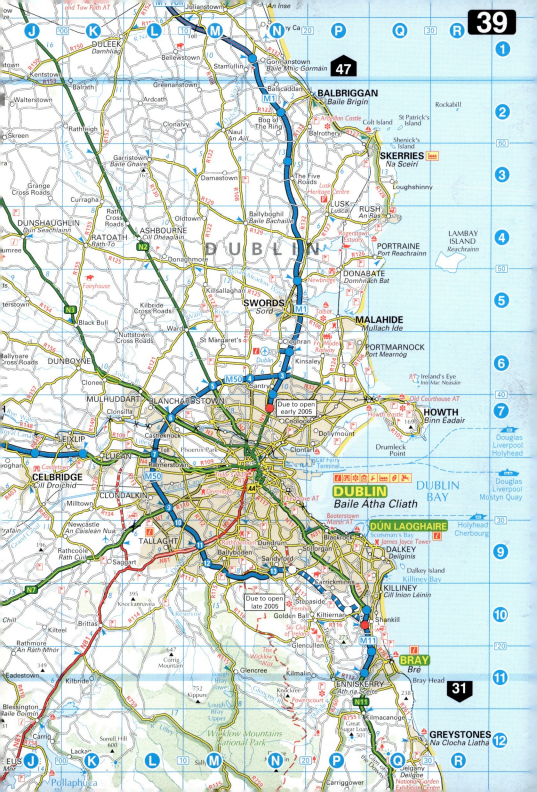

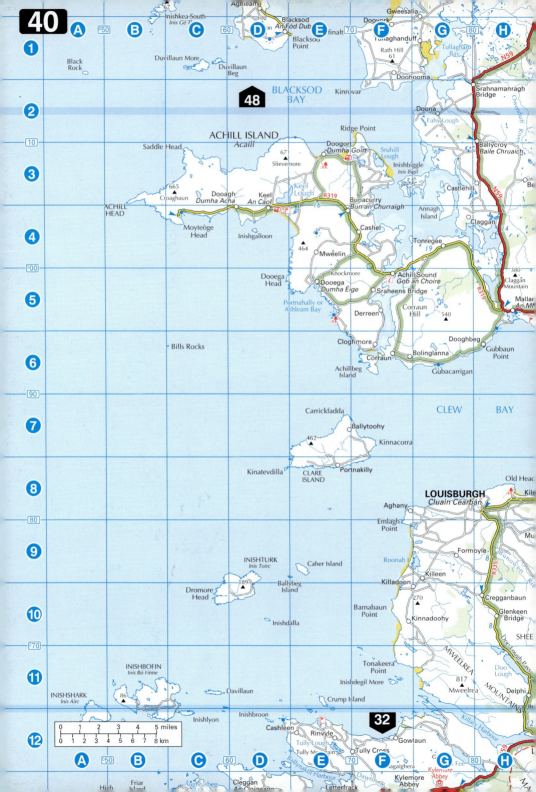

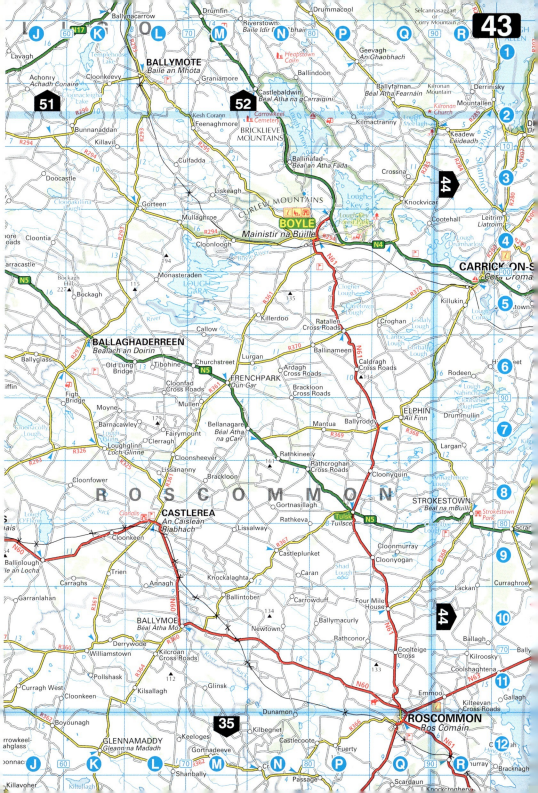

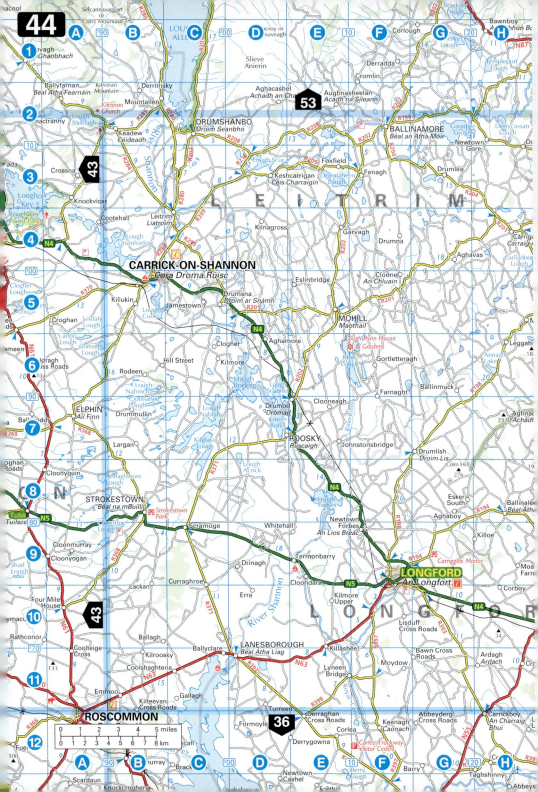

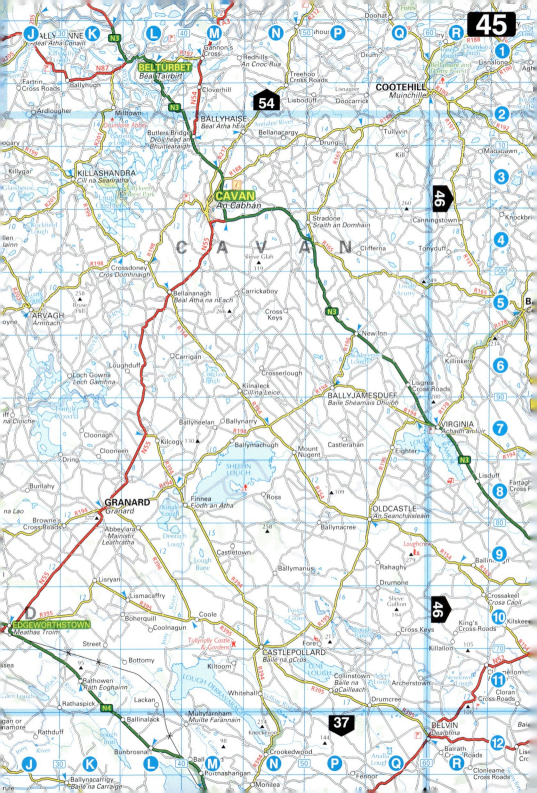

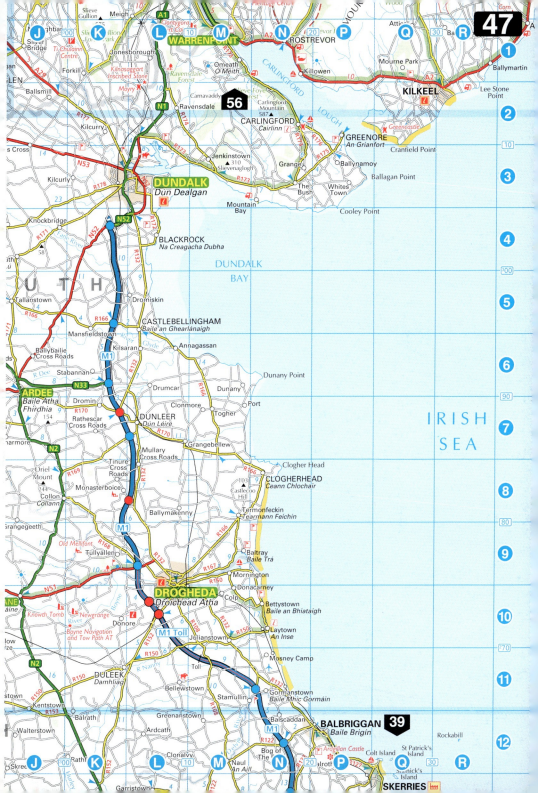

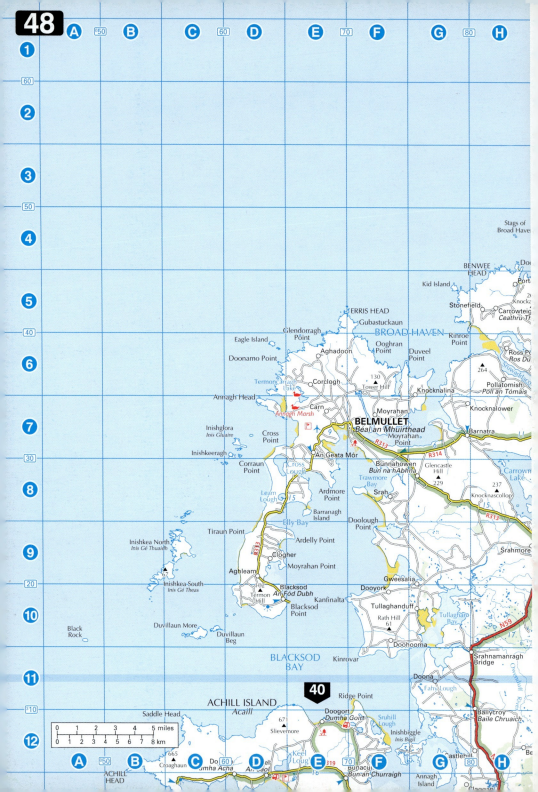

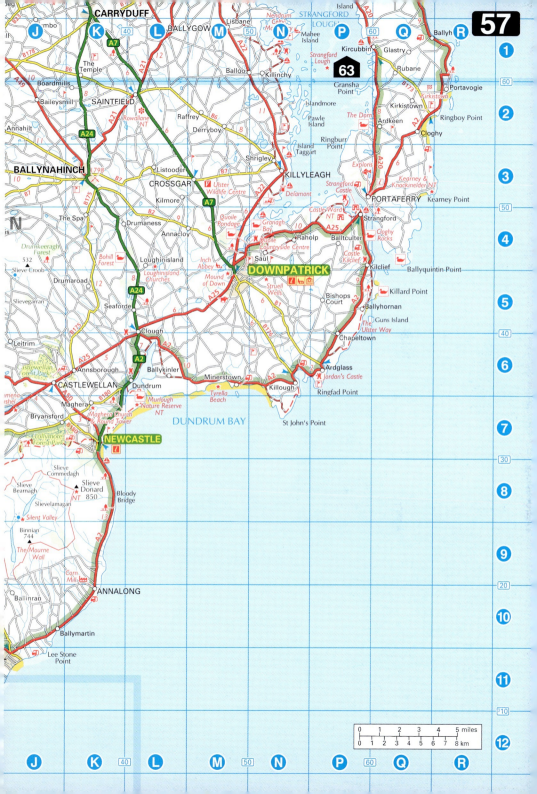

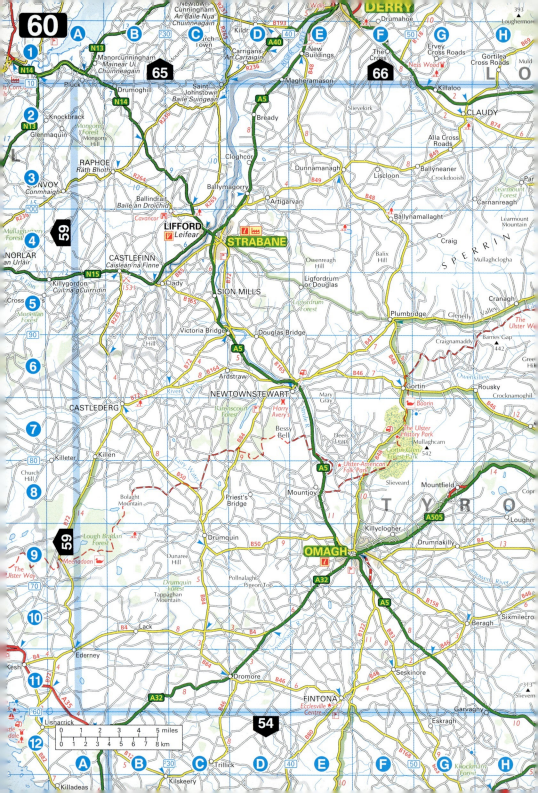

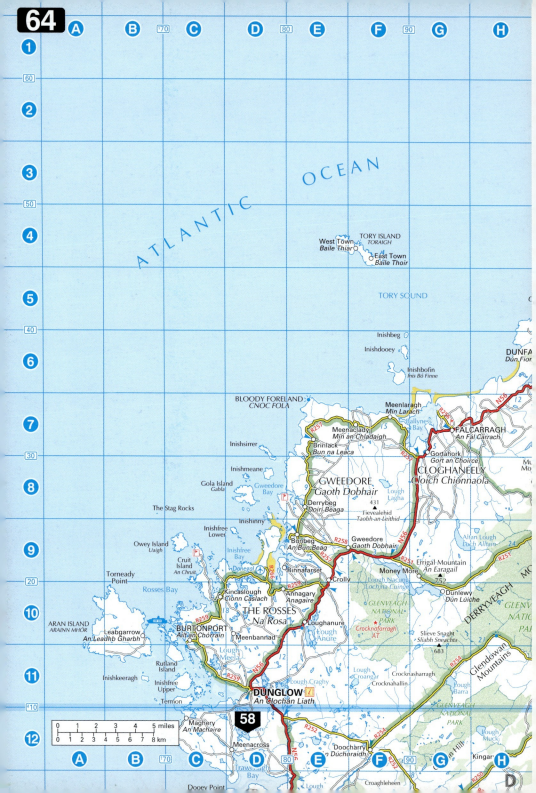

Counties and administrative areas

The index lists places appearing in the main-map section of the atlas in alphabetical order. The reference before each name gives the atlas page number and grid reference of the square in which the place appears. The map shows counties and other internal administration areas in each country, together with a list of the abbreviated county name forms used in the index.

50 places of interest are indexed in red, airports in blue.

Northern Ireland

Antrim	Antrim
Armagh	Armagh
Down	Down
Fermanagh	Antrim
Londonderry	Lderry
Tyrone	Tyrone

Republic of Ireland

Carlow	Carlow	**Leitrim**	Leitrm
Cavan	Cavan	**Limerick**	Limrck
Clare	Clare	**Longford**	Longfd
Cork	Cork	**Louth**	Louth
Donegal	Donegl	**Mayo**	Mayo
Dublin	Dublin	**Meath**	Meath
Dublin City (1)	Dublin	**Monaghan**	Monhan
Dún Laoghaire-		**Offaly**	Offaly
Rathdown (2)	Dublin	**Roscommon**	Roscom
Fingal (3)	Dublin	**Sligo**	Sligo
South Dublin (4)	Dublin	**Tipperary North**	Tippry
Galway	Galway	**Tipperary South**	Tippry
Kerry	Kerry	**Waterford**	Watfd
Kildare	Kildre	**Westmeath**	Wmeath
Kilkenny	Kilken	**Wexford**	Wexfd
Laois	Laois	**Wicklow**	Wicklw

A

26 H4 Abbey Galway
34 H6 Abbey Galway
36 G2 Abbeyderg Cross Roads Longfd
16 E11 Abbeydorney/Mainistir Ó dTorna Kerry
17 K10 Abbeyfeale/Mainistir na Féile Limrck
45 L9 Abbeylara/Mainistir Leathrátha Longfd
28 H9 Abbeyleix/Mainistir Laoise Laois
36 H3 Abbeyshrule/Mainistir Shruthla Longfd
19 J5 Abington Limrck
40 F5 Achill Sound/Gob an Choire Mayo
51 M11 Achonry/Achadh Conaire Sligo
42 F2 Aclare/Áth an Chláir Sligo
56 D5 Acton Armagh
22 F10 Adamstown Wexfd
11 Q6 Adara/Áth Dara Limrck
34 D8 Addergoole Galway
42 E7 Addergoole Mayo
3 M6 Adrigole/Eadargóil Cork
22 F8 Aghaboe Laois
44 G8 Aghaboy Longfd
1 K10 Aghabullogue Cork
53 L11 Aghacashel/Achadh an Chaisil Leitrm
E 9 Aghada Cork
42 H6 Aghadiffin Mayo
48 E6 Aghadoon Mayo
67 M9 Aghadowey Lderry
4 B10 Aghadown Cork
62 E11 Aghadagher Limrck
41 M8 Aghagower Mayo
42 E11 Aghalee Antrim
44 Q7 Aghamore Leitrm
42 Q7 Aghamore Mayo
40 F8 Aghany Mayo
31 J8 Aghavannagh Wicklw
42 H6 Aghavas Leitrm
34 F5 Agher Cross Roads Meath
12 E10 Aghern Cork
48 D9 Aghleam Mayo
45 J7 Aghnacliff/Achadh na Cloiche Longfd
8 F11 Aghnagar Bridge Kerry
5 L4 Aghnamarroge Cross Roads Cork
55 K10 Aghnamullen Monhan
67 M9 Agivey Bridge Lderry
8 G6 Aglish Kerry
27 M6 Aglish Tippry
7 K3 Aglish Watfd
11 M8 Ahadallane Cross Roads Cork
16 E7 Ahafona Kerry
3 N9 Ahakista Cork
35 N7 Ahascragh/Áth Eascrach Galway
L 3 Aherla Cork
12 E5 Ahnaseed Bridge Tippry
62 D3 Ahoghill Antrim
F8 Aldergrove Antrim
60 C3 Alla Cross Roads Lderry
38 E10 Allen Kildre
38 E9 Allenwood/Fiodh Alúine Kildre
2 G7 Allihies/Na hAilíchí Cork
55 P4 Allistragh Armagh
35 L7 Alloon Lower Galway
22 F2 Altamont Gardens Carlow
59 N4 Altnapaste Donegl
48 E7 An Geata Mór Mayo
8 H5 Anascaul/Abhainn an Scáil Kerry
1 D4 Anglesborough Limrck
19 M4 Anglesey Bridge Tippry
54 G8 Anlore Monhan
26 C10 Annacarriga Clare
19 N6 Annacarty Tippry
56 F5 Annaclone Down
57 M4 Annacloy Down
18 C4 Annacotty Limrck
31 K10 Annacurragh Wicklw
8 H5 Annagap Kerry
64 D10 Annagary/Anagaire Donegl
14 L6 Annagassan Louth
18 H4 Annagh Limrck
43 J4 Annagh Roscom
24 F10 Annagh Cross Roads Clare
34 C7 Annaghdown/Eanach Dhúin Galway
26 D9 Annaghneal Clare
18 D2 Annagore Bridge Clare
56 H2 Annahilt Down
77 K10 Annalong Down
1 L6 Annamoe/Áth na mBó Wicklw
55 M9 Annayalla Monhan
10 H4 Anne's Bridge Cork
18 E7 Annestown Watfd
20 B3 Annfield Tippry
57 K6 Annsborough Down
62 F6 Antrim Antrim
2 C11 Araglin Cork
12 E8 Araglin Bridge Kilken
24 D3 Aran Islands Galway
45 Q11 Archerstown Wmeath
46 F6 Ardagh Meath
17 N8 Ardagh/Ardach Limrck
44 H11 Ardagh/Ardach Longfd
43 N6 Ardagh Cross Roads Roscom
37 K9 Ardan Offaly
38 D5 Ardanew Meath
58 F5 Ardara/Ard an Ratha Donegl
22 F2 Ardattin Carlow
59 N6 Ardbane Donegl
62 B8 Ardboe Tyrone
39 L2 Ardcath Meath
16 C11 Ardconnell Kerry
27 L8 Ardcrony Tippry
3 L4 Ardea Bridge Kerry
47 J6 Ardee/Baile Átha Fhirdhia Louth
16 C11 Ardfert/Ard Fhearta Kerry
5 J9 Ardfield Cork
13 J5 Ardfinnan/Ard Fhíonáin Tippry
6 E5 Ardglass Cork
57 P6 Ardglass Down
3 J5 Ardgroom/Dhá Dhrom Cork

2 F4 Ardkearagh Kerry
57 Q2 Ardkeen Down
34 C2 Ardkill Mayo
28 H7 Ardlea Laois
54 B11 Ardlougher Cavan
7 L6 Ardmore/Aird Mhór Watfd
37 L7 Ardmoney Wmeath
18 F3 Ardnacrusha Clare
34 G6 Ardnasodan Galway
18 G11 Ardpatrick Limrck
6 E3 Ardra Cork
4 B7 Ardrah Cork
4 C6 Ardrah Cork
26 C3 Ardrahan/Ard Raithin Galway
55 Q2 Ardress Armagh
29 P6 Ardscull Cross Roads Kildre
60 C6 Ardstraw Tyrone
61 P8 Ardtrea Tyrone
4 H8 Argideen Bridge Cork
31 M11 Arklow/An tInbhear Mór Wicklw
19 J5 Arless Laois
55 P4 Armagh Armagh
68 B7 Armoy Antrim
53 Q6 Arney Ferman
10 Q6 Arraagh Limrck
14 G6 Arthurstown Wexfd
67 K7 Articlave Lderry
60 D3 Artigarvan Tyrone
45 J5 Arvagh/Armhach Cavan
39 L4 Ashbourne/Cill Dhéagláin Meath
17 N11 Ashford Limrck
31 N6 Ashford/Áth na Fuinseoige Wicklw
20 G6 Ashill Tippry
23 J4 Askamore Wexfd
31 J9 Askanagap Wicklw
5 P4 Askeaton/Eas Geitine Limrck
16 F6 Astee Kerry
38 D2 Athboy/Baile Átha Buí Meath
12 K8 Athea/Áth an tSléibhe Limrck
34 H9 Athenry/Baile Átha an Rí Galway
30 D3 Athgarvan Kildre
18 F9 Athlacca Limrck
37 K6 Athleague/Áth Liag Roscom
36 D6 Athlone/Baile Átha Luain Wmeath
36 E6 Athlone Castle Wmeath
20 D3 Athnid Tippry
29 N7 Áth Bhfia/Áth Fhia Í Kildre
20 H10 Attanagh Laois
56 H10 Attical Down
35 P10 Atticoffey Galway
35 M7 Attireppan Galway
42 C2 Attymass/Áit Tí an Mheasaigh Mayo
35 J8 Attymon/Áth Tiomáin Galway
41 Q4 Aucloggeen Galway
34 E7 Aucloggeen Galway
9 J3 Aughacasla Kerry
54 H3 Augher Tyrone
15 L5 Aughfad Wexfd
3 L6 Aughils Kerry
62 B2 Aughnacleagh Antrim
55 K3 Aughnacloy Tyrone
53 M11 Aughnasheelan/Acadh na Sileann Leitrm
25 N6 Aughrim Clare
35 N9 Aughrim/Eachroim Galway
31 K10 Aughrim/Eachroim Wicklw
31 M10 Avoca/Abhóca Wicklw

B

38 E6 Baconstown Meath
22 C3 Bagenalstown/Muine Bheag Carlow
24 D5 Baile an Teampall Clare
57 J2 Baileysmill Down
24 C6 Bailieborough/Coill an Choillagin Cavan
39 P2 Balbriggan/Baile Brigín Dublin
51 N4 Balinfull Sligo
42 C8 Balla Mayo
26 C5 Ballaba Galway
55 J9 Ballady Cork
34 C2 Ballagh Galway
17 N10 Ballagh Limrck
36 B4 Ballagh Roscom
37 J2 Ballagh Roscom
19 Q6 Ballagh Tippry
22 F10 Ballagh Wexfd
43 K6 Ballaghaderreen/Bealach an Doirín Roscom
17 K10 Ballaghbehy Limrck
62 E7 Ballaghboy Tippry
23 K8 Ballaghkeen Wexfd
28 D7 Ballaghmore Laois
52 E3 Ballaghnatrillick Sligo
37 K10 Ballard Offaly
22 H2 Ballard Cross Roads Wicklw
26 C5 Ballardiggan Galway
15 Q3 Balleen Kilken
21 J2 Balleen Kilken
29 N9 Ballickmoyler Laois
22 B9 Balliniloge Kilken
26 H11 Ballina Tippry
37 L4 Ballina Wmeath
50 E10 Ballina/Béal an Átha Mayo
5 P4 Ballinaboy Cork
32 K5 Ballinaboy Galway
37 Q6 Ballinabrackey Meath
29 N11 Ballinabranagh Carlow
31 L8 Ballinaclash Wicklw
5 N6 Ballinadee Cork
37 M10 Ballinagar Offaly
53 K3 Ballinagleragh Leitrm
19 J2 Ballinahinch Laois
5 P4 Ballinalack Wmeath
31 N6 Ballinalea Wicklw
44 H8 Ballinalee/Béal Átha na Lao Longfd
54 B3 Ballinamallard Ferman
21 K4 Ballinamara Cross Roads Kilken
43 P6 Ballinameen Roscom
35 N5 Ballinamore Bridge Galway

5 K7 Ballinascarty Cork
35 Q8 Ballinasloe/Béal Átha na Sluaighe Galway
12 H9 Ballinaspick Watfd
9 Q6 Ballinashet Cork
15 L3 Ballinaslay Wexfd
16 E10 Ballinclohar Cross Roads Kerry
5 N2 Ballincollig/Baile an Chollaigh Cork
27 M4 Ballincrea Kilken
14 E5 Ballincrea Kilken
6 D5 Ballincurrig Cork
27 F6 Ballindaggan Cork
12 C7 Ballindangan Cork
25 N2 Ballinderreen/Baile an Dorin Galway
27 L6 Ballinderry Tippry
42 E11 Ballindine/Baile an Daighin Mayo
52 F10 Ballindoon Sligo
60 C4 Ballindrait/Baile an Droichid Donegl
8 D5 Ballineanig Kerry
4 H6 Ballineen/Béal Átha Fhinin Cork
43 N3 Ballinfad/Béal an Átha Fada Sligo
1 Q7 Ballingarrane Limrck
27 N6 Ballingarry Limrck
6 G2 Ballingarry/Baile an Gharrai Tippry
18 C8 Ballingary/Baile an Gharrai Limrck
4 E3 Ballingeary/Béal Átha an Chaortnaigh Cork
31 J10 Ballinglen Wicklw
4 G7 Ballingurteen Cork
30 H9 Ballinhassig Cork
54 F10 Ballinkillin Carlow
22 C4 Ballinkillin Carlow
28 C8 Ballinleeny Limrck
6 E4 Ballinlough Kerry
46 B9 Ballinlough Meath
43 J9 Ballinlough/Baile an Locha Roscom
6 C10 Ballinluska Cork
44 F2 Ballinmore/Béal an Átha Mór Leitrm
44 G6 Ballinmuck Longfd
5 K8 Ballinorcher Cork
57 J10 Ballinran Down
8 D4 Ballinrannig Kerry
27 M10 Ballinree Tippry
6 B9 Ballinreeshig Cork
33 Q2 Ballinrobe/Baile an Róba Mayo
26 P8 Ballinruan Clare
2 D3 Ballinskelligs/Baile an Sceilge Kerry
5 N7 Ballinspittle/Béal Átha an Spidéil Cork
41 P9 Ballintober Roscom
43 M10 Ballintober Roscom
57 Q5 Ballintober/Baile an Tóchair Sligo
67 Q5 Ballintoy Antrim
50 K10 Ballintra/Baile an tSratha Donegl
29 M7 Ballintubbert Laois
20 E6 Ballinunty Tippry
20 E6 Ballinure Tippry
13 Q3 Ballinurra Tippry
27 P11 Ballinvarry Kilken
5 J4 Ballinveny Tippry
25 N2 Ballinvronig Cork
30 C6 Ballitore/Béal Átha an Tuair Kildre
38 C4 Ballivor/Baile Íomhair Meath
22 E2 Ballon/Balana Carlow
63 M11 Balloo Down
52 F13 Balloor Leitrm
56 B11 Ballsmill Armagh
57 P4 Ballturter Down
58 H11 Ballure Donegl
18 C7 Ballvea Cork
12 D6 Ballyaghaderg Bridge Cork
8 D10 Ballyagran Limrck
17 Q8 Ballyalinan Limrck
47 J6 Ballybaile Cross Roads Louth
35 M6 Ballybaun Galway
55 L9 Ballybay/Béal Átha Beithe Monhan
46 F3 Ballybay Cross Roads Monhan
13 K5 Ballybeg Tippry
37 P10 Ballybeg Tippry
39 M9 Ballyboden Dublin
59 P5 Ballybofey/Bealach Feich Donegl
38 B6 Ballyboggan Meath
59 N4 Ballyboghil/Baile Bachaille Dublin
62 B9 Ballyboy Antrim
36 F6 Ballybornia Wmeath
8 F5 Ballybower Kerry
28 D3 Ballyboy Offaly
3 N11 Ballybrack Kerry
2 E5 Ballybrack Cork
38 C7 Ballybrack Kerry
7 J4 Ballybrack Watfd
20 D2 Ballybristy Tippry
29 L4 Ballybrit Laois
16 D11 Ballybroman Kerry
18 H6 Ballybrood Limrck
28 E9 Ballybrophy/Baile Uí Bhroithe Laois
18 D3 Ballybroughan Clare
37 Q7 Ballybryan Offaly
16 C9 Ballybunnion/Baile an Bhuinneánaigh Kerry
30 C9 Ballybunny Cork
19 K2 Ballycahane Tippry
20 C4 Ballycahill Tippry
23 L5 Ballycallan Kilken
21 K5 Ballycanew/Baile Uí Chonnmhaí Wexfd
13 K5 Ballycar Clare
22 H6 Ballycarney Wexfd
62 D2 Ballycarry Antrim
67 J7 Ballycastle Antrim
68 C5 Ballycastle Antrim
49 P6 Ballycastle/Baile an Chaisil Mayo
62 H5 Ballyclare Antrim

44 C11 Ballyclare Roscom
20 E10 Ballyclerahan Tippry
11 L5 Ballycolgy/Baile Cloch Cork
15 N6 Ballycogly Wexfd
28 Q9 Ballycolla Laois
24 Q8 Ballycommaun Cork
27 K9 Ballycommon Tippry
29 K11 Ballycommon Kilken
32 D6 Ballyconneely/Baile Conaola Galway
54 B10 Ballyconnell/Béal Átha Conaill Cavan
17 N2 Ballycorick Bridge Clare
6 G9 Ballycotton/Baile Choitín Cork
27 L3 Ballycroy Galway
40 H2 Ballycroy/Baile Chruaich Mayo
7 M3 Ballycullane Watfd
14 H6 Ballycullane/Baile Uí Choileáin Wexfd
31 M6 Ballycullen Wicklw
36 H8 Ballycumber/Béal Átha Chomair Offaly
7 L4 Ballycurrane Watfd
12 Q6 Ballydaly Cork
10 F7 Ballydaly Cork
36 B8 Ballydangan Roscom
6 F9 Ballydavid Cork
26 G2 Ballydavid Galway
8 D4 Ballydavid/Baile na nGall Kerry
29 K5 Ballydavis Laois
3 Q9 Ballydehob/Béal an Dá Chab Cork
12 C7 Ballydeloughy Cork
10 E5 Ballydesmond/Baile Deasumhan Cork
2 G8 Ballydonegan Cork
26 G2 Ballydoogan Galway
11 Q5 Ballydoyle Cork
14 C7 Ballyduff Watfd
23 J5 Ballyduff Wexfd
6 E4 Ballyduff/An Baile Dubh Kerry
12 G9 Ballyduff/An Baile Dubh Watfd
31 M5 Ballyduff Cross Roads Wicklw
12 G7 Ballyeafy Watfd
22 H5 Ballyeaston Antrim
27 Q5 Ballyeighter Offaly
8 E5 Ballyeightragh Kerry
23 M2 Ballyfad Wexfd
42 E8 Ballyfarnagh Mayo
52 H11 Ballyfarnan/Baile Átha Fearnáin Roscom
14 E3 Ballyfasy Kilken
6 B10 Ballyfeard Cork
8 D5 Ballyferriter/Baile an Fheirtéaraigh Kerry
23 L5 Ballyfin Wexfd
28 G5 Ballyfin/An Baile Fionn Laois
35 P5 Ballyforan/Béal Átha Feoráinne Roscom
37 Q8 Ballyfore Offaly
21 M3 Ballyfoyle Kilken
63 K2 Ballygalley Antrim
35 N4 Ballygar/Béal Átha Ghártha Galway
13 R9 Ballygarran Watfd
14 B7 Ballygarran Watfd
23 N6 Ballygarrett Wexfd
42 B10 Ballygarries Mayo
55 J2 Ballygawley Tyrone
52 E8 Ballygawley/Baile Uí Dhalaigh Sligo
12 E6 Ballyglbin Cork
12 G6 Ballyglass Mayo
43 J6 Ballyglass Mayo
34 C6 Ballyglass Mayo
66 C2 Ballygorman Donegl
23 L7 Ballygortin Wexfd
63 L11 Ballygowan Down
11 K4 Ballygrady Cork
19 Q7 Ballygriffin Tippry
22 B8 Ballygub Kilken
18 F10 Ballyguba Limrck
14 G6 Ballyhack Wexfd
30 D10 Ballyhacket Cross Roads Carlow
17 L6 Ballyhaght Limrck
17 L6 Ballyhahill Limrck
45 M2 Ballyhaise/Béal Átha hÉis Cavan
63 Q11 Ballyhalbert Down
18 A4 Ballyhale Galway
21 M8 Ballyhale/Baile Héil Kilken
19 N2 Ballyhane Cross Roads Tippry
5 N3 Ballyhank Cork
42 Q9 Ballyhaunis/Béal Átha hAmhnais Mayo
41 P8 Ballyhean Mayo
12 G6 Ballyhickey Clare
22 H9 Ballyhickey Clare
14 E4 Ballyhomuck Kilken
10 H5 Ballyhoolahan Cork
12 B9 Ballyhooly/Baile Átha hÚlla Cork
57 P5 Ballyhornan Down
54 C10 Ballyhugh Cavan
57 P9 Ballyhugh Cavan
9 P12 Ballyhuppahane Cork
45 P6 Ballyjamesduff/Baile Shéamais Dhuibh Cavan
37 N10 Ballykeal Offaly
21 K5 Ballykeefe Cross Roads Kilken
56 H3 Ballykeel Down
30 E6 Ballykean Wmeath
66 Q9 Ballykelly Lderry
38 B9 Ballykilleen Offaly
14 D6 Ballykilty Cork
57 L6 Ballykinler Down
14 E7 Ballykinsella Watfd

Coolnagun - Enniskean

73

45 L10 Coolnagun Wmeath
39 N7 Coolock Dublin
28 E7 Coolrain Laois
23 M7 Coolroe Wexfd
27 N3 Coolross Tippry
6 B9 Coolsallagh Cork
44 C11 Coolshaghtena Roscom
43 Q11 Coolteige Cross Roscom
8 G9 Coomduff Kerry
3 Q5 Coomhola Bridge Cork
4 D6 Coomleagh Cork
18 E4 Coonagh Limrck
54 F5 Cooneen Ferman
43 M4 Coonloogh Sligo
16 H3 Cooraclare/Cuar an Chláir Clare
21 P3 Coorleagh Kilken
3 Q9 Coosane Cork
43 Q4 Cootehall Roscom
55 J11 Coothill/Muinchille Cavan
11 M5 Copsetown Cross Roads Cork
16 E3 Corbally Clare
50 G8 Corbally Sligo
30 D3 Corbally Cross Roads Kildre
44 H10 Corboy Longfd
48 E6 Corclogh Mayo
46 H4 Corcreeghagh Louth
49 M11 Corcullin Mayo
10 C4 Cordal Kerry
41 M9 Cordarragh Mayo
38 E9 Corduff Kildre
5 Q2 Cork/Corcaigh Cork
5 Q3 Cork Cork
68 B9 Corkey Antrim
36 E2 Corlea Longfd
26 F6 Corlea Bridge Clare
42 D3 Corlee Mayo
53 P10 Corlough Cavan
36 C7 Cornafulla Roscom
33 M4 Cornamona/Corr na Móna Galway
42 B10 Cornanagh Mayo
37 L9 Corndarragh Offaly
36 F9 Corr Hill Offaly
26 F7 Corrakyle Clare
55 Q6 Corran Cross Roads Armagh
34 D7 Corrandulla Galway
40 F6 Corraun Mayo
62 F2 Correen Antrim
37 Q5 Correlistown Wmeath
22 C4 Corries Cross Carlow
34 F6 Corrofin Galway
25 L8 Corrofin/Cora Finne Clare
53 K9 Corry Leitrm
21 K4 Corstown Cross Roads Kilken
46 E10 Cortown Meath
49 N8 Corvoley Mayo
33 L9 Costelloe/Casla Galway
8 H5 Coumduff Kerry
12 F8 Countygate Watfd
15 J3 Courthoyle Wexfd
5 M8 Courtmacsherry/Cúirt Mhic Shéafraidh Cork
17 P7 Courtmatrix Limrck
23 M4 Courtown/Baile na Cúirte Wexfd
4 D5 Cousane Cork
23 K3 Craan Wexfd
23 K4 Craanford Wexfd
31 K9 Crafield Wicklw
24 H4 Craggagh Clare
26 D9 Cragroe Clare
64 G4 Craig Tyrone
67 M11 Craigavole Lderry
56 D2 Craigavon Armagh
62 C2 Craigs Antrim
62 C2 Craigs Cross Antrim
60 H5 Cranagh Tyrone
23 J7 Crane Wexfd
65 M7 Cranford Donegl
17 L3 Cranny Clare
61 N6 Cranny Lderry
18 D3 Cratloe Clare
34 H10 Craughwell/Creachmhaoil Galway
63 M7 Crawfordsburn Down
37 N3 Crazy Corner Wmeath
4 C10 Creagh Cork
55 N8 Creaghanroe Monhan
11 L9 Crean's Cross Roads Cork
18 E6 Crecora Limrck
16 H2 Creegh Clare
35 N2 Creegs Galway
65 K7 Creeslough/An Craoslach Donegl
49 P7 Creevagh Mayo
17 P6 Creeves Limrck
25 J4 Cregg Clare
4 G10 Cregg Cork
55 Q10 Creggan Armagh
36 E9 Creggan Offaly
61 J8 Creggan Tyrone
40 H10 Creggанbaun Mayo
29 L10 Crettyard Laois
66 H8 Crindle Lderry
27 Q5 Crinkill Offaly
58 G7 Croagh Donegl
18 C7 Croagh Limrck
59 F9 Crockets Town Mayo
37 N8 Croghan Offaly
43 Q5 Croghan Roscom
64 E9 Crolly Donegl
9 L6 Cromane Kerry
53 N10 Cromlin Leitrm
28 G7 Cromoge Cross Roads Laois
16 E9 Crompaun Bridge Kerry
37 N2 Crookedwood Wmeath
3 M11 Crookhaven/An Cruachán Cork
5 K3 Crookstown Cork
30 D6 Crookstown Kildre
18 E7 Croom/Cromadh Limrck
16 C5 Cross Clare
7 K4 Cross Watfd
33 Q3 Cross/An Chrois Mayo
5 N4 Cross Barry Cork
45 N5 Cross Keys Cavan
45 Q10 Cross Keys Meath
5 L6 Cross Mahon Cork
59 Q5 Cross Roads Donegl
15 N3 Crossabeg Wexfd
46 B10 Crossakeel/Crosa Caoil Meath
42 D10 Crossboyne Mayo
35 P10 Crossconnell Galway
45 L4 Crossdoney/Cros Domhnaigh Cavan
44 H11 Crossea Longfd
45 N6 Crosserlough Cavan
57 M3 Crossgar Down
67 L8 Crossgare Lderry
6 C9 Crosshaven/Bun an Tábhairne Cork
29 N4 Crosskeys Kildre
55 Q10 Crossmaglen Armagh
50 C10 Crossmolina/Crois Mhaoilíona Mayo
43 Q3 Crossna Roscom
25 N3 Crossooha Galway
20 G2 Crosspatrick Kilken
23 K2 Crosspatrick Wicklw
6 G6 Crowbally Cork
62 F8 Crumlin Antrim
3 J6 Crumpane Cork
25 N8 Crusheen/Croisín Clare
29 K9 Crutt Kilken
28 F9 Cuffsborough Cross Roads Laois
41 Q3 Cuilkillew Mayo
62 G11 Culcavy Down
66 E4 Culdaff/Cúil Dabhcha Donegl
43 L3 Culfadda Sligo
66 E3 Culkeeny Donegl
28 G11 Cullahill/An Chúlchoill Laois
12 C4 Cullane Limrck
55 P11 Cullaville Armagh
18 C2 Culleen Clare
50 H8 Culleens Sligo
10 F6 Cullen Cork
19 L8 Cullen Tippry
12 B6 Cullenagh Cork
15 K7 Cullenstown Wexfd
42 D3 Cullin Mayo
4 B8 Cullomane Cross Roads Cork
62 D2 Cullybackey Antrim
55 Q9 Cullyhanna Armagh
66 D9 Culmore Lderry
38 H5 Culmullin Cross Roads Meath
61 P3 Culnady Lderry
12 F9 Currabeha Cork
23 K10 Curracloe Wexfd
5 J4 Curraclogh Cork
7 L6 Curragh Watfd
30 C3 Curragh Camp Kildre
43 J11 Curragh West Galway
39 K3 Curragha Meath
4 F7 Curraghalicky Cork
36 B5 Curraghboy Roscom
31 J11 Curraghlawn Wicklw
21 P9 Curraghmore Kilken
27 J11 Curraghmore Tippry
44 C9 Curraghroe Roscom
12 G10 Curraglass Cork
28 B9 Curragunneen Tippry
61 P4 Curran Lderry
9 Q4 Currans Kerry
19 N3 Curreeny Tippry
10 A5 Currow Kerry
42 G3 Curry Sligo
68 E8 Cushendall Antrim
68 F7 Cushendun Antrim
29 L2 Cushina Offaly

D

37 N9 Daingean/An Daingean Offaly
39 Q9 Dalkey/Deilginis Dublin
13 N8 Dalligan Bridge Watfd
37 M6 Dalystown Wmeath
39 M3 Damastown Dublin
67 M8 Damhead Lderry
21 M6 Danesfort Kilken
6 G5 Dangan Cork
20 B8 Dangandargan Tippry
22 H8 Darby's Gap Wexfd
55 P7 Darkley Armagh
55 J10 Dartry Monhan
22 G8 Davidstown Wexfd
49 M10 Deel Bridge Mayo
31 N3 Delgany/Deilgne Wicklw
40 H11 Delphi Mayo
38 B2 Delvin/Dealbhna Wmeath
10 G6 Dernagree Cork
53 N10 Derradda Leitrm
25 L11 Derragh Clare
36 E2 Derraghan Cross Roads Longfd
24 F8 Derreen Clare
8 F11 Derreen Kerry
40 F5 Derreen Mayo
41 N3 Derreen Mayo
3 N6 Derreenacarrin Cork
4 B9 Derreenard Cork
2 H4 Derreenauliff Kerry
3 L7 Derreeny Cork
37 J9 Derries Offaly
38 C9 Derries Offaly
36 C8 Derrineel Roscom
53 J11 Derrinisky Roscom
38 D8 Derrinturn Kildre
66 C10 Derry City Walls Lderry
62 C11 Derryadd Armagh
64 E8 Derrybeg/Doirí Beaga Donegl
57 M2 Derryboy Down
26 E5 Derrybrien Galway
4 E8 Derryclogh Cork
28 F5 Derrycon Laois
36 H10 Derrycooly Offaly
28 D2 Derrydolney Offaly
20 F2 Derryfadda Tippry
4 E2 Derryfineen Cork
19 K3 Derrygareen Tippry
29 J4 Derrygile Laois
37 L8 Derrygolan Wmeath
53 N3 Derrygonnelly Ferman
36 E2 Derrygowna Longfd
13 K4 Derrygrath Tippry
37 M9 Derrygrogan Offaly
67 P7 Derrykeighan Antrim
36 C8 Derrylahan Roscom
54 B8 Derrylin Ferman
62 C11 Derrymacash Armagh
9 L3 Derrymore Kerry
4 E5 Derrynacaheragh Cork
33 J7 Derryrush/Doire Iorrais Galway
33 J4 Derryvoreada Galway
43 K10 Derrywode Galway
67 P7 Dervock Antrim
6 D4 Desert Cork
61 P5 Desertmartin Lderry
53 Q4 Devenish Ferman
8 E5 Dingle/An Daingean Kerry
62 H6 Doagh Antrim
65 N5 Doagh Beg Donegl
27 L11 Dolla Tippry
56 E2 Dollingstown Down
39 P7 Dollymount Dublin
39 P5 Donabate/Domhnach Bat Dublin
47 M10 Donacarney Meath
38 F8 Donadea Kildre
54 D8 Donagh Ferman
63 P8 Donaghadee Down
56 E3 Donaghcloney Down
28 E9 Donaghmore Laois
39 L4 Donaghmore Meath
61 M10 Donaghmore Tyrone
46 F10 Donaghpatrick Meath
22 E9 Donard Wexfd
30 F6 Donard/Dún Ard Wicklw
19 P7 Donaskeagh Tippry
59 K8 Donegal/Dún na nGall Donegl
64 D9 Donegal Donegl
59 K8 Donegal Castle Donegl
11 N4 Doneraile/Dún ar Aill Cork
19 N7 Donohill Tippry
38 D4 Donore Meath
47 K10 Donore Meath
11 L9 Donoughmore Cork
40 D4 Dooagh/Dumha Acha Mayo
49 N9 Doobehy Mayo
54 G11 Doocarrick Cavan
43 J3 Doocastle Mayo
59 J2 Doocharry/An Dúchoraidh Donegl
40 E5 Dooega/Dumha Éige Mayo
44 H3 Doogary Cavan
40 H6 Dooghbeg Mayo
40 E3 Doogort/Dumha Goirt Mayo
55 M9 Doohamlat Monhan
54 H9 Doohat Monhan
48 F10 Doohooma Mayo
49 M10 Dooleeg Mayo
24 G6 Doolin/Dúlainn Clare
35 N7 Doon Galway
12 G7 Doon Tippry
19 L5 Doon/Dún Limrck
36 F8 Doon Cross Roads Offaly
40 G2 Doona Mayo
16 E5 Doonaha Clare
16 G2 Doonbeg Clare
8 G6 Doonmanagh Kerry
32 G6 Doonreaghan Galway
14 C6 Doornane Kilken
48 F10 Dooyork Mayo
3 L11 Dough Cork
34 D9 Doughiska Galway
6 B8 Douglas/Dúglas Cork
60 D6 Douglas Bridge Tyrone
20 C3 Dovea Tippry
14 B4 Dowling Kilken
67 J6 Downhill Lderry
65 K6 Downies/Na Dúnaibh Donegl
12 D8 Downing Cork
57 M5 Downpatrick Down
53 K8 Dowra/An Damhshraith Cavan
36 D6 Doyle's Bridge Roscom
20 G7 Drangan/Drongán Tippry
61 M5 Draperstown Lderry
61 J3 Dreen Lderry
16 B9 Dreenagh Kerry
9 M2 Drehidasillagh Kerry
4 E8 Driminidy Cork
28 F6 Drimmo Laois
4 D7 Drimoleague/Drom Dhá Liag Cork
4 F8 Drinagh Cork
32 D5 Drinagh Galway
44 D9 Drinagh Roscom
15 P5 Drinagh Wexfd
50 G7 Drinaghan Sligo
45 J7 Dring Longfd
11 L11 Dripsey Cork
3 P9 Drishane Bridge Cork
47 L10 Drogheda/Droichead Átha Louth
8 G3 Drom Kerry
20 C2 Drom Tippry
10 H6 Dromagh Cork
52 G7 Dromahair/Droim Dhá Thiar Leitrm
9 K9 Dromalonhurt Bridge Kerry
56 H4 Dromara Down
8 G11 Dromaragh Kerry
11 P9 Dromboy South Cork
18 B11 Dromcolliher/Drom Collachair Limrck
16 D11 Dromcunnig Kerry
11 P9 Dromgarriff Cork
18 G9 Dromin Limrck
47 K7 Dromin Louth
11 L2 Dromina/Drom Aidhne Cork
27 K8 Dromineer Tippry
47 L5 Dromiskin Louth
11 M7 Drommahane Cork
3 M9 Dromnea Cork
4 C7 Dromore Cork
56 G3 Dromore Down
60 D11 Dromore Tyrone
7 K3 Dromore Watfd
51 J7 Dromore West Sligo
10 H10 Dromree Cross Roads Cork
17 L11 Dromtrasna Limrck
54 H10 Drum Monhan
36 C7 Drum Roscom
66 D10 Drumahoe Lderry
55 P10 Drumakill Monhan
26 D7 Drumandoora Clare
57 K4 Drumaness Down
25 K10 Drumanure Clare
51 M7 Drumard Sligo
57 K5 Drumaroad Down
27 J2 Drumatober Galway
19 Q4 Drumbane Tippry
19 K2 Drumbaun Tippry
63 J10 Drumbeg Down
63 J11 Drumbo Down
47 L6 Drumcar Louth
26 D9 Drumcharley Clare
25 M9 Drumcliff Clare
52 D5 Drumcliff/Droim Chliabh Sligo
46 G7 Drumcondra/Droim Conrach Meath
45 Q11 Drumcree Wmeath
22 D4 Drumfea Carlow
52 E9 Drumfin Sligo
66 B6 Drumfree Donegl
34 D7 Drumgriftin Galway
59 L7 Druminnin Donegl
26 G4 Drumkeary Galway
59 Q3 Drumkeen Donegl
53 J9 Drumkeeran/Droim Caorthainn Leitrm
44 G3 Drumlea Leitrm
44 G7 Drumlish/Droim Lis Longfd
36 D8 Drumlosh Roscom
52 F9 Drummacool Sligo
24 G11 Drummin Clare
41 K10 Drummin Mayo
44 B7 Drummullin Roscom
44 F4 Drumna Leitrm
60 G9 Drumnakilly Tyrone
44 E7 Drumod/Dromad Leitrm
60 B2 Drumoghill Donegl
45 Q10 Drumone Meath
60 C9 Drumquin Tyrone
36 G5 Drumraney Wmeath
38 H4 Drumree Meath
13 J9 Drumroe Watfd
44 C2 Drumshanbo/Droim Seanbhó Leitrm
33 P3 Drumsheel Mayo
44 C5 Drumsna/Droim ar Snámh Leitrm
67 J10 Drumsurn Lderry
45 P2 Drung Cavan
17 J9 Duagh/Dubháth Kerry
20 D7 Dually Tippry
39 N8 Dublin Dublin
39 N6 Dublin Dublin
38 C7 Duffy's Cross Roads Kildre
36 C7 Duggarry Roscom
47 K11 Duleek/Damhliag Meath
39 P9 Dún Laoghaire Dublin
62 G7 Dunadry Antrim
65 Q4 Dunaff Donegl
35 N2 Dunamon Roscom
47 M6 Dunany Louth
21 N5 Dunbell Kilken
39 K6 Dunboyne Meath
38 E10 Dunbyrne Kildre
14 G7 Duncannon/Dún Canann Wexfd
15 L7 Duncormick Wexfd
47 L3 Dundalk/Dún Dealgan Louth
5 N6 Dunderrow Cork
38 F2 Dunderry Meath
55 K4 Dundian Monhan
63 L9 Dundonald Down
35 N8 Dundoogan Galway
62 G8 Dundrod Antrim
57 L6 Dundrum Down
39 N9 Dundrum Dublin
19 P6 Dundrum/Dún Droma Tippry
65 J6 Dunfanaghy/Dún Fionnachaidh Donegl
38 E7 Dunfierth Cross Roads Kildre
61 M11 Dungannon Tyrone
14 F4 Dunganstown Wexfd
21 P6 Dungarvan Kilken
13 N10 Dungarvan/Dún Garbhán Watfd
61 K2 Dungiven Lderry
64 D11 Dunglow/An Clochán Liath Donegl
6 F6 Dungourney Cork
14 C8 Dunhill Watfd
26 H4 Duniry Galway
27 Q9 Dunkerrin Offaly
58 G8 Dunkineely/Dún Cionnaola Donegl
14 D5 Dunkitt Kilken
30 E5 Dunlavin/Dún Luáin Wicklw
47 L7 Dunleer/Dún Léire Louth
64 G10 Dunlewy/Dún Lúiche Donegl
67 Q10 Dunloy Antrim
67 N5 Dunluce Castle Antrim
3 M10 Dunmanus Cork
4 F6 Dunmanway/Dún Mánmhaí Cork
6 H4 Dunmoon Watfd
34 H2 Dunmore/Dún Mór Galway
14 F8 Dunmore East/Dún Mór Watfd
62 H10 Dunmurry Antrim
21 L8 Dunnamaggan Kilken
60 E3 Dunnamanagh Tyrone
61 K7 Dunnamore Tyrone
21 L4 Dunningstown Kilken
8 C5 Dunquin/Dún Chaoin Kerry
38 H3 Dunsany Cross Roads Meath
39 J4 Dunshaughlin/Dún Seachlainn Meath
28 H10 Durrow/Darú Laois
3 P8 Durrus/Dúras Cork
35 Q5 Dysart Roscom
37 L5 Dysart Wmeath

E

39 J11 Eadestown Kildre
20 G5 Earlshill Tippry
50 H6 Easky/Iascaigh Sligo
53 K6 East Barrs Leitrm
64 F4 East Town/Baile Thoir Donegl
63 L6 Eden Antrim
38 B8 Edenderry/Eadan Doire Offaly
59 R11 Ederney Ferman
45 J10 Edgeworthstown/Meathas Troim Longfd
66 E9 Eglinton Lderry
55 M2 Eglish Tyrone
45 Q7 Eighter Cavan
43 Q7 Elphin/Ail Finn Roscom
18 H9 Elton Limrck
26 D2 Emlagh Cross Roads Galway
2 E2 Emlaghmore Kerry
19 K9 Emly/Imleach Tippry
44 B11 Emmoo Roscom
29 K4 Emo/Ioma Laois
55 K5 Emyvale/Scairb na gCaorach Monhan
25 M10 Ennis/Inis Clare
22 H8 Enniscorthy/Inis Córthaidh Wexfd
5 J6 Enniskean/Inis Céin Cork

74 Enniskerry - Julianstown

31 M2 Enniskerry/Áth na Sceire Wicklw
53 Q5 Enniskillen Ferman
24 H8 Ennistimon/Inis Díomáin Clare
24 C3 Eochaill Clare
44 D10 Erra Roscom
41 L11 Erriff Bridge Mayo
28 D10 Errill Laois
66 E11 Ervey Cross Roads Lderry
54 G6 Eshnadarragh Ferman
34 H9 Esker Galway
44 G8 Esker South Longfd
49 M10 Eskeragh Bridge Mayo
9 L11 Eskine Kerry
54 G2 Eskragh Tyrone
44 E5 Eslinbridge Leitrm
2 H6 Eyeries/Na hAorai Cork
27 M2 Eyrecourt/Dún an Uchta Galway

F

9 P6 Faha Kerry
13 Q8 Faha Glen Watfd
10 B3 Fahaduff Kerry
9 J2 Fahamore Kerry
65 Q8 Fahan Donegl
8 C6 Fahan Kerry
12 C4 Fahanasoodry Limrck
27 L3 Fahy Galway
35 M9 Fahy Galway
25 N9 Fair Green Clare
36 G6 Fairfield Wmeath
43 L7 Fairymount Roscom
64 G7 Falcarragh/An Fál Carrach Donegl
24 H4 Fanore More Clare
11 Q3 Farahy Cork
36 E7 Fardrum Wmeath
9 P3 Farmer's Bridge Kerry
36 G7 Farnagh Wmeath
44 F6 Farnaght Leitrm
4 E5 Farnanes Cork
5 L3 Farnanes Cork
14 E4 Farnoge Kilken
5 L3 Farran Cork
28 G9 Farran Cross Roads Laois
9 Q5 Farranfore/An Fearann Fuar Kerry
46 C8 Fartagh Cross Roads Cavan
54 B11 Fartrin Cross Roads Cavan
26 E8 Feakle/An Fhiacail Clare
24 B3 Fearann an Choirce Clare
18 F7 Fedamore/Feadamair Limrck
16 C5 Feeard Clare
25 J4 Feenagh Clare
18 C10 Feenagh Limrck
43 M2 Feenaghmore Sligo
61 J2 Feeny Lderry
44 F3 Fenagh Leitrm
9 L2 Fenit/An Fhianait Kerry
22 D3 Fennagh Carlow
14 C8 Fennor Watfd
37 P2 Fennor Wmeath
17 P10 Feohanagh Limrck
8 D4 Feohanagh/An Fheothanach Kerry
3 M3 Feoramore Kerry
36 F10 Ferbane/An Féar Bán Offaly
12 D9 Fermoy/Mainistir Fhear Maí Cork
23 J6 Ferns/Fearna Wexfd
18 D5 Ferry Bridge Limrck
31 N11 Ferrybank Wicklw
20 F9 Fethard/Fiodh Ard Tippry
14 H8 Fethard/Fiodh Ard Wexfd
13 Q7 Fews Watfd
19 K3 Fiddane Tippry
14 B4 Fiddown/Fiodh Dúin Kilken
9 Q5 Fieries Kerry
43 J7 Figh Bridge Roscom
13 Q4 Figlash Tippry
25 L3 Finavarra Clare
45 M8 Finnea/Fiodh an Átha Wmeath
56 H4 Finnis Down
33 M3 Finny Mayo
60 E11 Fintona Tyrone
59 K3 Fintown/Baile na Finne Donegl
16 G9 Finuge/Fionnúig Kerry
67 P10 Finvoy Antrim
2 F8 Firkeel Cork
24 G6 Fisherstreet Clare
62 H5 Five Corners Antrim
28 B3 Fivealley Offaly
52 F6 Fivemilebourne Leitrm
5 Q4 Fivemilebridge Cork
54 E4 Fivemiletown Tyrone
26 E7 Flagmount Clare
21 P4 Flagmount Kilken
33 J7 Flannery Bridge Galway
9 J5 Flemingstown Kerry
53 P7 Florence Court NT Ferman
8 G9 Foilmore Bridge Kerry
3 Q10 Foilnamuck Cork
18 G10 Foley's Cross Roads Limrck
29 P5 Fontstown Kildre
46 D11 Fordstown Meath
45 P10 Fore Wmeath
56 C10 Forkill Armagh
25 J4 Formoyle Clare
25 J10 Formoyle Clare
36 D2 Formoyle Longfd
40 G9 Formoyle Mayo
11 M9 Fornaght Cork
18 E10 Fort Middle Limrck
36 E3 Forthill Longfd
6 C7 Fota Wildlife Park Cork
15 K5 Foulkesmill Wexfd
20 E7 Foulkstown Tippry
25 M10 Fountain Cross Clare
43 Q10 Four Mile House Roscom
35 Q4 Four Roads Roscom
44 E3 Foxfield Leitrm
42 C4 Foxford/Béal Easa Mayo
17 N5 Foynes/Faing Limrck
11 J3 Freemount/Cillín an Chrónáin Cork
43 M6 Frenchpark/Dún Gar Roscom
21 K3 Freshford/Achadh Úr Kilken
30 E6 Freynestown Wicklw
18 F6 Friarstown Limrck
58 H7 Frosses/Na Frosa Donegl
35 P2 Fuerty Roscom
25 M4 Funshin More Galway
3 P6 Furkeal Cork
13 P7 Furraleigh Watfd
17 L2 Furroor Clare
12 E6 Furrow Cork
9 M5 Fybagh Kerry

G

16 H7 Gabbett's Bridge Kerry
37 M5 Gainstown Wmeath
22 G10 Galbally Wexfd
19 K10 Galbally/An Gallbhaile Limrck
20 D5 Galbertstown Tippry
16 G8 Galey Cross Roads Kerry
62 D3 Galgorm Antrim
44 C11 Gallagh Roscom
28 E11 Galmoy Kilken
27 Q3 Galros Cross Roads Offaly
38 G4 Galtrim Meath
34 D9 Galway/Gaillimh Galway
34 E9 Galway Galway
19 L4 Gannavane Limrck
54 E10 Gannon's Cross Cavan
38 G5 Garadice Meath
35 P8 Garbally Demense Galway
13 J4 Garnavilla Tippry
37 P7 Garr Offaly
42 G11 Garrafrauns Galway
49 P8 Garranard Mayo
11 N2 Garrane Cross Roads Cork
5 J4 Garranereagh Cork
43 J10 Garranlahan Roscom
16 F4 Garraun Clare
27 J3 Garraun Galway
9 P4 Garraun Kerry
30 E9 Garrettstown Carlow
53 J3 Garrison Ferman
39 L3 Garristown/Baile Gháire Dublin
6 F4 Garrycaheragh Cork
50 D10 Garrycloonagh Mayo
15 J6 Garrycullen Wexfd
67 P9 Garryduff Antrim
18 E10 Garryfine Limrck
22 D4 Garryhill Carlow
27 J9 Garrykennedy Tippry
6 H7 Garrymore Cork
27 N10 Garrynafana Tippry
6 G8 Garryvoe Cork
67 L10 Garvagh Lderry
44 E4 Garvagh Leitrm
14 H2 Garvaghy Tyrone
19 J10 Garyspillane Limrck
21 J2 Gattabaun Kilken
37 N5 Gaybrook Wmeath
37 N10 Geashill/Géisill Offaly
52 G10 Geevagh/An Ghaobhach Sligo
46 F9 Georges Cross Roads Meath
14 A8 Georgestown Watfd
3 N8 Gerahies Cork
67 N5 Giant's Causeway NT Antrim
46 F10 Gibstown Meath
56 D4 Gilford Down
46 H6 Glack Cross Roads Louth
3 P10 Glan Cork
4 G4 Glan Cross Roads Cork
3 M9 Glanalin Cork
9 K8 Glanbehy Bridge Kerry
4 C7 Glandart Cork
4 F9 Glandore/Cuan Dor Cork
53 M8 Glangevlin Cavan
3 N8 Glanlough Cork
6 B7 Glanmire/Gleann Maghair Cork
16 F10 Glanoe Kerry
3 L9 Glanroon Cork
11 L7 Glantane Cork
12 C8 Glanworth/Gleannúir Cork
68 B11 Glarryford Antrim
28 E10 Glasha Cross Roads Laois
8 D4 Glashabeg Kerry
11 Q8 Glashaboy East Cork
11 P8 Glashaboy North Cork
16 H11 Glashananoon Kerry
17 K7 Glashapullagh Limrck
46 D4 Glasleck Cavan
55 L5 Glaslough/Glasloch Monhan
36 E5 Glassan/Glasán Wmeath
63 Q11 Glastry Down
66 H7 Glebe Lderry
65 L7 Glen Donegl
61 N3 Glen Lderry
6 G4 Glenacroghery Cork
52 G4 Glenade Leitrm
27 N9 Glenahilty Tippry
49 K7 Glenamoy/Gleann na Muaidhe Mayo
68 E9 Glenariff or Waterfoot Antrim
68 G11 Glenarm Antrim
62 F9 Glenavy Antrim
9 K7 Glenbeigh/Gleann Beithe Kerry
53 J6 Glenboy Leitrm
23 J8 Glenbrien Wexfd
12 B3 Glenbrohane Limrck
9 L9 Glencar Kerry
52 F5 Glencar/Gleann an Chairthe Leitrm
58 B7 Glencolumbkille/Gleann Cholm Cille Donegl
34 B4 Glencorrib Mayo
39 M11 Glencree Wicklw
39 N10 Glencullen Dublin
31 M4 Glendarragh Wicklw
16 B10 Glenderry Kerry
6 E5 Glendine Bridge Cork
65 J11 Glendowan/Gleann Domhain Donegl
26 D8 Glendree Clare
12 E6 Glenduff Cork
68 E7 Glendun Viaduct Antrim
31 M7 Glenealy Wicklw
49 P7 Glenedagh Mayo
66 E5 Gleneely/Gleann Daoile Donegl
53 L6 Glenfarne Leitrm
10 C8 Glenflesk Kerry
3 P5 Glengarriff/An Gleann Garbh Cork
6 G3 Glengoura Cork
66 G10 Glenhead Lderry
61 J6 Glenhull Tyrone
40 H10 Glenkeen Bridge Mayo
59 R2 Glenmaquin Donegl
17 K2 Glenmore Clare
14 F4 Glenmore/An Gleann Mhór Kilken
20 D10 Glennagat Tippry
10 F3 Glennaknockane Cork
35 K2 Glennamaddy/Gleann na Madadh Galway
10 F4 Glennamucklagh East Cork
13 R6 Glennaphuca Cross Roads Watfd
34 E9 Glennascaul Galway
63 K4 Glenoe Antrim
19 P5 Glenough Lower Tippry
19 P5 Glenough Upper Tippry
12 B5 Glenroe Limrck
6 F4 Glentane Cork
58 H5 Glenties/Na Gleannta Donegl
66 D5 Glentogher Donegl
33 L6 Glentrasna/Gleann Trasna Galway
67 Q11 Glenvale Antrim
65 P7 Glenvar Donegl
65 K10 Glenveagh Castle Donegl
6 B4 Glenville/Gleann an Phréacháin Cork
17 K6 Glin/An Gleann Limrck
43 M11 Glinsk Galway
32 G7 Glinsk/Glinsce Galway
6 C7 Glounthaune Cork
63 L4 Glynn Antrim
22 C8 Glynn Carlow
15 M3 Glynn Wexfd
10 D6 Gneevgullia Kerry
19 Q8 Golden/An Gabhailín Tippry
39 P10 Golden Ball Dublin
3 M11 Goleen/An Góilín Cork
20 B6 Goold's Cross Tippry
22 B5 Goresbridge/An Droichead Nua Kilken
23 M4 Gorey/Guaire Wexfd
13 J5 Gormanstown Tippry
47 N11 Gormanstown/Baile Mhic Cormáin Meath
26 C5 Gort/An Gort Galway
24 B4 Gort na gCapall Clare
61 K8 Gortaclady Tyrone
3 K3 Gortagowan Kerry
64 G7 Gortahork/Gort an Choirce Donegl
20 B2 Gortalough Tippry
27 N3 Gortarevan Offaly
7 J6 Gortaroo Cork
53 N6 Gortatole Ferman
61 L8 Gorteagh Tyrone
35 K7 Gorteen Galway
29 L10 Gorteen Kilken
18 C10 Gorteen Limrck
43 L3 Gorteen Sligo
7 M4 Gorteen Watfd
28 F2 Gorteen Bridge Offaly
14 E6 Gorteens Kilken
27 J6 Gorteeny Galway
2 H6 Gortgarriff Cork
52 G7 Gortgarrigan Leitrm
10 B4 Gortglass Kerry
66 F11 Gortilea Cross Roads Lderry
60 F6 Gortin Tyrone
44 F6 Gortletteragh Leitrm
4 D4 Gortloughra Bridge Cork
33 K7 Gortmore Galway
49 P6 Gortmore Mayo
35 M2 Gortnadeeve Galway
21 J4 Gortnagap Cross Roads Kilken
17 M4 Gortnahaha Clare
66 H11 Gortnahey Lderry
20 G4 Gortnahoo Tippry
4 F4 Gortnahoughtee Cork
49 N9 Gortnahurra Mayo
9 Q2 Gortnaleaha Kerry
26 C8 Gortnamearacaun Clare
43 N8 Gortnasillagh Roscom
9 L8 Gortrelig Kerry
25 N4 Gortskeagh Galway
3 M8 Gouladoo Cork
2 H8 Gour Bridge Cork
32 F2 Gowlaun Galway
22 D7 Gowlin Carlow
21 P5 Gowran/Gabhrán Kilken
62 D3 Gracehill Antrim
18 G11 Graigue Cross Roads Limrck
13 P7 Graiguearush Watfd
22 C7 Graiguenamanagh/Gráig na Manach Kilken
30 H5 Granabeg Wicklw
45 K8 Granard/Gránard Longfd
30 D9 Graney Kildre
38 B7 Grange Kildre
14 B5 Grange Kilken
21 L5 Grange Kilken
47 N3 Grange Louth
13 K4 Grange Tippry
7 L5 Grange Watfd
15 M7 Grange Wexfd
52 D4 Grange/An Ghráinseach Sligo
29 N3 Grange Beg Kildre
28 E9 Grange Beg Laois
17 P8 Grange Bridge Limrck
30 D7 Grange Con Wicklw
39 J3 Grange Cross Roads Meath
47 L7 Grangebellew Louth
30 D11 Grangeford Carlow
47 J8 Grangegeeth Meath
52 E10 Graniamore Sligo
26 C3 Grannagh Galway
61 M11 Granville Tyrone
28 E9 Green Cross Roads Laois
31 K8 Greenan Wicklw
55 J8 Greenans Cross Roads Monhan
39 M2 Greenanstown Meath
60 H7 Greencastle Tyrone
66 G5 Greencastle/An Caisleán Nua Donegl
63 K6 Greenisland Antrim
47 P2 Greenore/An Grianfort Louth
11 N9 Grenagh Cork
63 P10 Greyabbey Down
17 K2 Greygrove Clare
66 F9 Greysteel Lderry
55 M2 Greystone Tyrone
31 N3 Greystones/Na Clocha Liatha Wicklw
12 B4 Griston Limrck
36 G8 Grogan Offaly
63 N7 Groomsport Down
53 L7 Gubaveeny Cavan
14 B6 Guilcagh Cross Roads Watfd
61 P4 Gulladuff Lderry
10 D6 Gullaun Kerry
52 G5 Gurteen Leitrm
14 H5 Gusserane Wexfd
64 E9 Gweedore/Gaoth Dobhair Donegl
48 G9 Gweesalia Mayo
6 E9 Gyleen Cork

H

47 J2 Hackballs Cross Louth
30 G9 Hacketstown/Baile Haicéid Carlow
5 P4 Halfway Cork
14 F7 Halfway House Watfd
46 F11 Halltown Cross Roads Meath
55 Q5 Hamiltonsbawn Armagh
62 H9 Hannahstown Antrim
21 M10 Harristown Kilken
34 C5 Headford/Áth Cinn Galway
10 C8 Headfort Kerry
15 M6 Heavenstown Cross Roads Wexfd
16 C9 Heirhill Kerry
63 M7 Helen's Bay Down
18 H7 Herbertstown/Baile Hiobaird Limrck
36 E10 Highstreet Offaly
6 D4 Hightown Cork
38 C5 Hill of Down Meath
44 B6 Hill Street Roscom
62 H11 Hillhall Down
56 G2 Hillsborough Down
56 G8 Hilltown Down
15 K5 Hilltown Wexfd
15 N6 Hilltown Wexfd
17 P5 Hogan's Bridge Limrck
19 N5 Hollyford Tippry
23 L3 Hollyfort Wexfd
26 D4 Hollymount Galway
42 C11 Hollymount Mayo
30 F4 Hollywood/Cillín Chaoimhín Wicklw
18 G8 Holycross Limrck
20 C5 Holycross/Mainistir na Croiche Tippry
53 M6 Holywell Ferman
63 L8 Holywood Down
14 G9 Hook Lighthouse Wexfd
46 E8 Horath Cross Roads Meath
15 P6 Horetown Wexfd
20 E5 Horse & Jockey/An Marcach Tippry
37 J7 Horseleap/Baile Átha an Urchair Offaly
19 J8 Hospital/An tOspidéal Limrck
39 Q7 Howth/Binn Éadair Dublin
21 M9 Hugginstown Kilken
18 F4 Hunt Museum Limrck
18 C3 Hurlers Cross Clare

I

9 K6 Illaunstookagh Kerry
25 K9 Inagh/Eidhneach Clare
6 E9 Inch Cork
6 H5 Inch Cork
65 Q9 Inch Donegl
19 N4 Inch Tippry
23 M2 Inch Wexfd
9 K5 Inch/Inse Kerry
29 L6 Inch Cross Roads Laois
17 L10 Inchabaun Limrck
38 D5 Inchamore Bridge Meath
21 K2 Inchbeg Kilken
10 C11 Inchee Bridge Kerry
4 F5 Inchicahan Cross Roads Cork
4 F3 Inchigeelagh/Inse Geimhleach Cork
12 B8 Inchinapallas Cork
12 G5 Inchnamuck Tippry
5 M5 Inishannon/Inis Eonáin Cork
50 F8 Inishcrone/Inis Crabhann Sligo
61 Q3 Inishrush Lderry
46 H3 Iniskeen/Inis Caoin Monhan
21 P8 Inistioge/Inis Tíog Kilken
38 E6 Innfield/An Bóthar Buí Meath
58 H8 Inver/Inbhear Donegl
33 M10 Inveran/Indreabhán Galway
29 P3 Irish National Stud Kildre
42 F11 Irishtown Mayo
53 Q2 Irvinestown Ferman
58 H6 Ivy Bridge Donegl

J

31 N9 Jack White's Cross Roads Wicklw
29 L4 Jamestown Laois
44 C5 Jamestown Leitrm
21 L2 Jenkinstown Kilken
47 M3 Jenkinstown Louth
56 D7 Jerrettspass Armagh
14 G5 John F. Kennedy Ancestral Home Wexfd
42 E5 Johnsfort Mayo
44 E7 Johnstonsbridge Longfd
6 B8 Johnstown Cork
38 H10 Johnstown Kildre
46 G11 Johnstown Meath
15 L6 Johnstown Wexfd
31 L11 Johnstown Wicklw
31 N10 Johnstown Wicklw
20 G2 Johnstown/Baile Sheáin Kilken
38 E7 Johnstown Bridge Kildre
15 N5 Johnstown Castle Wexfd
21 N3 Johnswell Kilken
56 D10 Jonesborough Armagh
47 M10 Julianstown Meath

Kanturk - Lackan 75

K

11 J5 Kanturk/Ceann Toirc Cork
9 P8 Kate Kearney's Cottage Kerry
56 G5 Katesbridge Down
44 B2 Keadew/Céideadh Roscom
55 N7 Keady Armagh
3 K2 Kealariddig Kerry
3 J7 Kealincha Bridge Cork
4 B5 Kealkill Cork
4 E4 Kealvaugh Cork
33 Q8 Keeagh/An Chaothach Galway
40 D4 Keel/An Caol Mayo
8 G10 Keelnagore Kerry
35 L2 Keeloges Galway
41 M2 Keenagh Mayo
36 F2 Keenagh/Caonach Longfd
13 K10 Keereen Watfd
30 C11 Kellistown Cross Roads Carlow
62 E4 Kells Antrim
8 H8 Kells Kerry
21 L7 Kells/Ceanannas Kilken
46 D9 Kells/Ceanannas Meath
29 M11 Kelly's Bridge Kilken
30 F8 Kelshabeg Wicklw
3 P2 Kenmare/Neidín Kerry
27 Q4 Kennedy's Cross Roads Offaly
47 J11 Kentstown Meath
15 N5 Kerloge Wexfd
9 Q5 Kerry Kerry
9 N3 Kerry the Kingdom Kerry
17 N7 Kerryikyle Limrck
59 Q11 Kesh Ferman
44 D3 Keshcarrigan/Ceis Charraigín Leitrm
7 M5 Kiely's Cross Roads Watfd
16 B6 Kilbaha/Cill Bheathach Clare
30 C11 Kilballyhue Carlow
26 F11 Kilbane Clare
4 G3 Kilbarry Cork
14 D7 Kilbarry Watfd
26 C5 Kilbeacanty Galway
14 B8 Kilbeg Watfd
37 K7 Kilbeggan/Cill Bheagáin Wmeath
35 N2 Kilbegnet Roscom
12 E5 Kilbeheny Limrck
34 F3 Kilbenan Cross Roads Galway
29 N6 Kilberry Kildre
46 G10 Kilberry Meath
13 P5 Kilbrack Watfd
18 C6 Kilbreedy Limrck
18 F10 Kilbreedy Limrck
20 B7 Kilbreedy Tippry
33 K7 Kilbrickan/Cill Bhreacáin Galway
20 D2 Kilbrickane Tippry
28 G8 Kilbricken Laois
42 E5 Kilbride Mayo
38 E2 Kilbride Meath
30 H2 Kilbride Wicklw
31 N8 Kilbride Wicklw
39 L5 Kilbride Cross Roads Meath
12 C10 Kilbrien Cork
13 M8 Kilbrien Watfd
11 K4 Kilbrin Cork
5 M7 Kilbrittain/Cill Briotáin Cork
34 E10 Kilcaimin Galway
29 K2 Kilcappagh Offaly
58 D8 Kilcar/Cill Charthaigh Donegl
14 E7 Kilcaragh Cross Roads Watfd
30 H9 Kilcarney Wicklw
30 H9 Kilcarney Cross Roads Wicklw
16 H4 Kilcarroll Clare
20 H10 Kilcash Tippry
36 B8 Kilcashel Roscom
28 H2 Kilcavan Laois
26 E3 Kilchreest/Cill Chríost Galway
26 E8 Kilclaran Clare
57 P4 Kilclief Down
16 C6 Kilcloher Clare
37 M8 Kilclonfert Offaly
38 G7 Kilcock/Cill Choca Kildre
4 B10 Kilcoe Cork
45 L7 Kilcogy Cavan
14 E7 Kilcohan Watfd
34 F11 Kilcolgan/Cill Cholgáin Galway
5 K6 Kilcolman Cork
17 N7 Kilcolman Limrck
7 M5 Kilcolman Watfd
27 P7 Kilcomin Offaly
12 H4 Kilcommon Tippry
19 N3 Kilcommon Tippry
34 H10 Kilconierin Galway
34 E3 Kilconly Galway
35 M8 Kilconnell/Cill Chonaill Galway
11 P4 Kilconnor Cork
56 H7 Kilcoo Down
53 K4 Kilcoo Cross Roads Ferman
31 N4 Kilcoole/Cill Chomhghuill Wicklw
6 E4 Kilcor Cork
25 N6 Kilcorkan Clare
28 C3 Kilcormac/Cill Chormaic Offaly
10 H7 Kilcorney Cork
23 J8 Kilcotty Wexfd
6 H8 Kilcredan Cork
43 L11 Kilcroan Cross Roads Galway
3 M9 Kilcrohane Cork
6 G4 Kilcronat Cork
30 D4 Kilcullen/Cill Chuillinn Kildre
8 H3 Kilcummin Kerry
10 A6 Kilcummin Kerry
47 K3 Kilcurly Louth
47 K2 Kilcurry Louth
10 B3 Kilcusnaun Kerry
38 D3 Kildalkey Meath
29 N4 Kildangan Kildre
29 P3 Kildare/Cill Dara Kildre
22 F4 Kildavin/Cill Damháin Carlow
14 B7 Kildermody Watfd
18 D5 Kildimo New Limrck
18 D5 Kildimo Old Limrck
12 B6 Kildorrery/Cill Dairbhre Cork
61 M8 Kildress Tyrone
66 B11 Kildrum Donegl
8 D5 Kildurrihy Kerry
19 P8 Kilfeakle Tippry
16 E4 Kilfearagh Clare
25 J7 Kilfenora/Cill Fhionnúrach Clare
18 H11 Kilfinnane/Cill Fhionáin Limrck
18 D7 Kilfinny Limrck
16 E11 Kilflyn Kerry
10 B11 Kilgarvan/Cill Gharbháin Kerry
35 N6 Kilglass Galway
36 B3 Kilglass Roscom
50 G7 Kilglass Sligo
9 N7 Kilgobnet Kerry
13 M9 Kilgobnet Watfd
30 D5 Kilgowan Kildre
18 C6 Kilgrogan Limrck
29 P8 Kilkea Kildre
21 M9 Kilkeasy Kilken
16 E3 Kilkee/Cill Chaoi Clare
57 J11 Kilkeel Down
42 F6 Kilkelly/Cill Cheallaigh Mayo
21 M4 Kilkenny/Cill Chainnigh Kilken
21 M4 Kilkenny Castle Kilken
36 F5 Kilkenny West Wmeath
5 N7 Kilkerran Cork
35 K3 Kilkerrin Galway
32 H8 Kilkieran/Cill Chiaráin Galway
21 M3 Kilkieran Cross Roads Kilken
4 B10 Kilkilleen Cork
17 J11 Kilkinlea Lower Limrck
26 C11 Kilkishen/Cill Chisín Clare
45 Q3 Kill Cavan
32 D4 Kill Galway
14 B8 Kill Watfd
38 H10 Kill/An Chill Kildre
36 G6 Killachonna Wmeath
12 C6 Killaclug Cork
18 D10 Killacolla Limrck
53 Q3 Killadeas Ferman
35 P6 Killaderry Galway
40 G10 Killadoon Mayo
17 N4 Killadysert/Cill an Dísirt Clare
26 C6 Killafeen Galway
15 M7 Killag Wexfd
17 M9 Killaghteen Limrck
13 J9 Killahaly Watfd
21 J4 Killahy Cross Roads Kilken
50 E8 Killala/Cill Ala Mayo
46 B10 Killallon Meath
26 H11 Killaloe/Cill Dalua Clare
60 G2 Killaloo Lderry
21 J8 Killamery Kilken
37 J5 Killane Wmeath
26 D7 Killanena Clare
22 F7 Killann/Cill Anna Wexfd
16 G2 Killard Clare
52 H7 Killarga Leitrm
9 R7 Killarney/Cill Airne Kerry
37 J5 Killaroo Wmeath
45 K3 Killashandra/Cill na Seanrátha Cavan
44 E10 Killashee Longfd
42 E4 Killasser Mayo
33 M2 Killateeaun Mayo
28 B4 Killaun Offaly
41 P9 Killavally Mayo
6 F3 Killavarilly Cork
11 Q10 Killavarrig Cork
43 K3 Killavil Sligo
35 J3 Killavoher Galway
11 P6 Killavullen/Cill an Mhuilinn Cork
53 J5 Killea Leitrm
27 Q11 Killea Tippry
14 F8 Killea Watfd
62 F7 Killead Antrim
6 H6 Killeagh/Cill Ia Cork
24 C4 Killeany/Cill Éinne Clare
22 D5 Killedmond Carlow
12 C6 Killee Bridge Cork
17 N10 Killeedy Limrck
26 C7 Killeen Galway
40 G9 Killeen Mayo
27 P4 Killeen Tippry
61 P10 Killeen Tyrone
25 N2 Killeenaran Galway
20 B8 Killeenasteena Tippry
25 P3 Killeenavarra Galway
34 G11 Killeeneenmore Galway
4 C8 Killeenleagh Cork
11 Q10 Killeens Cross Cork
54 H8 Killeevan Monhan
35 Q6 Killeglan Roscom
37 L11 Killeigh/Cill Aichidh Offaly
60 A7 Killen Tyrone
23 M5 Killenagh Wexfd
29 L4 Killenard Laois
27 P4 Killenaule Tippry
20 F6 Killenaule/Cill Náile Tippry
43 N5 Killerdoo Roscom
30 D10 Killerrig Cross Roads Carlow
37 N8 Killeshil Offaly
29 N10 Killeshin Laois
59 R7 Killeter Tyrone
35 J11 Killilan Bridge Galway
16 H5 Killimer Clare
27 K3 Killimor/Cill Iomair Galway
25 L7 Killinaboy/Cill Iníne Baoith Clare
5 K2 Killinardrish Cork
14 C4 Killinaspick Kilken
63 N11 Killinchy Down
23 M8 Killincooly Wexfd
9 J3 Killiney Kerry
39 Q9 Killiney/Cill Iníon Léinín Dublin
15 P6 Killinick Wexfd
23 M2 Killinierin Wexfd
46 B6 Killinkere Cavan
25 N4 Killinny Galway
38 C10 Killinthomas Kildre
31 N5 Killiskey Wicklw
10 G11 Killnamartery/Cill na Martra Cork
44 H9 Killoe Longfd
50 D6 Killogeary Mayo
36 F7 Killogeenaghan Wmeath
2 D2 Killoluaig Kerry
25 P4 Killomoran Galway
37 P9 Killoneen Offaly
35 N10 Killoran Galway
9 M6 Killorglin/Cill Orglan Kerry
35 K6 Killoscobe Galway
57 N6 Killough Down
33 Q2 Killour Mayo
56 F10 Killowen Down
39 M5 Killsallaghan Dublin
37 Q4 Killucan/Cill Liúcainne Wmeath
44 B5 Killukin Roscom
37 K11 Killurin Offaly
15 M3 Killurin Wexfd
2 D3 Killurly Kerry
20 F9 Killusty Tippry
62 D4 Killybegs Antrim
58 F8 Killybegs/Na Cealla Beaga Donegl
60 F9 Killyclogher Tyrone
45 J3 Killygar Leitrm
59 R5 Killygordon/Cúil na gCuirridín Donegl
67 L10 Killykergan Lderry
55 M5 Killylea Armagh
57 N3 Killyleagh Down
55 L6 Killyneill Monhan
28 B4 Killyon Offaly
6 F8 Kilmacahill Cork
31 M3 Kilmacanoge Wicklw
11 M4 Kilmaclenine Cross Roads Cork
14 D5 Kilmacow/Cill Mhic Bhúith Kilken
65 L9 Kilmacrenan/Cill Mhic Réanáin Donegl
13 Q7 Kilmacthomas/Coill Mhic Thomáisín Watfd
43 P2 Kilmactranny Sligo
21 L9 Kilmaganny/Cill Mogeanna Kilken
34 C3 Kilmaine Mayo
46 E7 Kilmainham Wood Meath
25 L11 Kilmaley/Cill Mháile Clare
39 P11 Kilmalin Wicklw
18 G10 Kilmallock/Cill Mocheallóg Limrck
21 J5 Kilmanagh Kilken
17 J11 Kilmaniheen Kerry
36 B4 Kilmass Roscom
29 P6 Kilmead Kildre
14 C6 Kilmeadan Watfd
38 E10 Kilmeage Kildre
18 B10 Kilmeedy/Cill Míde Limrck
38 G3 Kilmessan/Cill Mheasáin Meath
2 E8 Kilmichael Cork
4 G3 Kilmichael Cork
17 K3 Kilmihil/Cill Mhicil Clare
11 P9 Kilmona Cork
4 B12 Kilmoon Cork
55 Q3 Kilmore Armagh
18 G2 Kilmore Clare
57 L3 Kilmore Down
16 D8 Kilmore Kerry
42 C4 Kilmore Mayo
44 C6 Kilmore Roscom
15 M7 Kilmore Wexfd
38 G5 Kilmore Cross Roads Meath
15 M8 Kilmore Quay Wexfd
44 E10 Kilmore Upper Longfd
17 J9 Kilmorna Kerry
29 N8 Kilmorony Laois
42 H6 Kilmovee Mayo
23 M7 Kilmuckridge/Cill Mhucraise Wexfd
14 B9 Kilmurrin Watfd
24 F11 Kilmurry Clare
5 J3 Kilmurry Cork
18 C10 Kilmurry Limrck
30 E8 Kilmurry Wicklw
18 D2 Kilmurry/Cill Mhuire Clare
17 K4 Kilmurry McMahon Clare
24 B3 Kilmurvy/Cill Mhuirbhigh Clare
22 G5 Kilmyshall Wexfd
13 J10 Kilnacarriga Watfd
18 E2 Kilnacreagh Clare
44 D4 Kilnagross Leitrm
35 N9 Kilnahown Galway
45 M6 Kilnaleck/Cill na Leice Cavan
23 L7 Kilnamanagh Wexfd
25 L9 Kilnamona/Cill na Móna Clare
5 M5 Kilpatrick Cork
18 F6 Kilpeacon Cross Roads Limrck
31 N4 Kilpedder Wicklw
8 E4 Kilquane Kerry
30 G11 Kilquiggin Wicklw
67 Q8 Kilraghts Antrim
15 Q6 Kilrane Wexfd
67 N11 Kilrea Lderry
58 G5 Kilrean Donegl
35 L10 Kilreekill Galway
34 D9 Kilroghter Galway
24 C4 Kilronan/Cill Rónáin Clare
44 B11 Kilroosky Roscom
19 L9 Kilross Tippry
16 G4 Kilrush/Cill Rois Clare
43 L11 Kilsallagh Galway
41 J8 Kilsallagh Mayo
47 L6 Kilsaran Louth
38 D7 Kilshanchoe Kildre
9 J2 Kilshannig Kerry
24 H7 Kilshanny Clare
13 N4 Kilsheelan Tippry
5 L7 Kilshinahan Cork
46 C10 Kilskeer Meath
54 B3 Kilskeery Tyrone
42 D7 Kiltamagh/Caillte Mach Mayo
41 N9 Kiltarsaghaun Mayo
26 C4 Kiltartan Galway
22 F6 Kiltealy/Cill Téile Wexfd
39 J10 Kilteel Kildre
19 J7 Kilteely/Cill Tíle Limrck
44 B11 Kilteevan Cross Roads Roscom
30 F9 Kiltegan Wicklw
23 J5 Kilthomas Cross Roads Wexfd
39 P10 Kiltiernan Dublin
25 P2 Kiltiernan Galway
37 L8 Kiltober Wmeath
36 C5 Kiltoom Roscom
45 M11 Kiltoom Wmeath
35 P10 Kiltormer Galway
35 J9 Kiltullagh/Cill Tulach Galway
53 K4 Kiltyclogher/Coillte Clochair Leitrm
20 H8 Kilvemnon Tippry
42 F11 Kilvine Mayo
6 H3 Kilwatermoy Watfd
63 K3 Kilwaughter Antrim
39 J8 Kilwoghan Kildre
12 D8 Kilworth/Cill Uird Cork
12 D7 Kilworth Camp Cork
37 J7 Kimalady Offaly
17 K6 Kinard Limrck
53 Q7 Kinawley Ferman
64 C10 Kincaslough/Cionn Caslach Donegl
50 C8 Kincon Mayo
18 F4 King John's Castle Limrck
46 B10 King's Cross Roads Meath
59 L2 Kingarrow Donegl
46 E5 Kingscourt/Dún an Rí Cavan
61 P8 Kingsmill Tyrone
52 G2 Kinlough/Cionn Locha Leitrm
40 F10 Kinnadoohy Mayo
37 Q5 Kinnegad/Cionn Átha Gad Wmeath
28 C4 Kinnitty/Cion Eitigh Offaly
5 P6 Kinsale/Cionn tSáile Cork
7 K6 Kinsalebeg Watfd
39 P6 Kinsaley Dublin
33 L8 Kinvarra Galway
25 N3 Kinvarra/Cinn Mharra Galway
4 G7 Kippagh Bridge Cork
63 Q11 Kircubbin Down
67 P8 Kirkhills Antrim
57 Q2 Kirkistown Down
10 F5 Kishkeam Cork
41 L8 Knappagh Mayo
8 E10 Knights Town Kerry
17 J5 Knock Clare
28 D8 Knock Tippry
42 E8 Knock/An Cnoc Mayo
42 G5 Knock International Mayo
25 L9 Knockacaurhin Clare
10 A6 Knockacullig Kerry
50 D10 Knockadangan Bridge Mayo
17 P8 Knockaderry Limrck
18 H8 Knockainy/Cnoc Áine Limrck
13 P5 Knockalafalla Watfd
43 N9 Knockalaghta Roscom
17 K3 Knockalough Clare
30 H9 Knockananna Wicklw
42 G9 Knockanarra Mayo
30 G7 Knockanarrigan Wicklw
4 H4 Knockane Cork
12 B5 Knockanevin Cork
50 D10 Knockanillaun Mayo
7 J4 Knockanore Watfd
17 J8 Knockanure Kerry
28 E8 Knockaroe Laois
54 H6 Knockatallan Monhan
12 E8 Knockatrasnane Cork
24 H9 Knockatullaghaun Clare
35 N11 Knockaun Galway
12 H8 Knockaunarast Watfd
16 H10 Knockaunbrack Kerry
9 L6 Knockaunnaglashy Kerry
9 K7 Knockaunroe Kerry
8 E5 Knockavrogeen Kerry
17 L9 Knockawahig Limrck
13 M7 Knockboy Watfd
26 E10 Knockbrack Clare
59 R2 Knockbrack Donegl
16 E11 Knockbrack Kerry
46 C4 Knockbride Cavan
47 J4 Knockbridge Louth
20 E8 Knockbrit Tippry
5 L7 Knockbrown Cork
5 N3 Knockburden Cork
16 F10 Knockburrane Cross Roads Kerry
61 P4 Knockcloghrim Lderry
36 B3 Knockcroghery/Cnoc an Chrochaire Roscom
18 F9 Knockdarnan Limrck
37 M3 Knockdrin Wmeath
11 M7 Knockdrislagh Cork
9 R3 Knockeen Cross Roads Kerry
10 F5 Knockeenadallane Cork
10 C2 Knockeencreen Kerry
24 G6 Knockfin Cross Roads Clare
13 K4 Knocklofty Tippry
19 J9 Knocklong Limrck
25 P8 Knockmael West Clare
28 G11 Knockmannon Cross Roads Kilken
42 B3 Knockmore Mayo
12 F10 Knockmourne Cork
41 M5 Knockmoyle Bridge Mayo
17 M6 Knocknabooly Limrck
10 D5 Knocknaboul Cross Kerry
68 E7 Knocknacarry Antrim
30 C9 Knocknacree Cross Roads Kildre
5 M6 Knocknacurra Cork
17 J11 Knocknagashel/Cnoc na gCaiseal Kerry
26 G9 Knocknagower Clare
10 E6 Knocknagree Cork
9 N2 Knocknahaha Kerry
24 G11 Knocknahila Clare
5 M3 Knocknahilan Cork
48 G6 Knocknalina Mayo
48 G7 Knocknalower Mayo
6 G7 Knocknaskagh Cork
24 H8 Knockpatrick Clare
6 C6 Knockraha Cork
9 J10 Knockroe Kerry
13 M9 Knockroe Watfd
5 J7 Knocks Cork
28 G5 Knocks Laois
5 J7 Knockskagh Cork
10 H3 Knockskavane Cork
21 M8 Knocktopher/Cnoc an Tóchair Kilken
15 L6 Knocktown Cross Roads Wexfd
43 Q3 Knockvicar Roscom
5 M6 Knoppoge Bridge Cork
11 P7 Knuttery Cork
29 L7 Kyle Laois
26 G4 Kylebrack Galway
19 L5 Kylegarve Limrck
36 B10 Kylemore Galway
32 F3 Kylemore Abbey Galway

L

26 C3 Laban Galway
17 L5 Labasheeda/Leaba Shíoda Clare
60 B10 Lack Ferman
4 D2 Lackabaun Cork
29 N3 Lackagh Kildre
27 J10 Lackamore Tippry
21 P3 Lackan Carlow
44 B9 Lackan Roscom
30 H3 Lackan Wicklw

45 L11 Lackan Wmeath
35 Q4 Lackan Roscom
5 J4 Lackareagh Cork
10 C2 Lackbrooder Kerry
22 D10 Lacken Wexfd
12 B10 Lackendarragh North Cork
28 D7 Lackey Laois
15 Q7 Lady's Island Wexfd
6 G7 Ladysbridge/Droichead na Scuab Cork
67 Q5 Lagavara Antrim
19 Q9 Lagganstown Tippry
61 N11 Laghey Corner Tyrone
59 K9 Laghy/An Lathaigh Donegl
11 L7 Laharan Cross Roads Cork
41 P11 Lahardaun/Leathardán Mayo
17 K5 Lakyle Clare
21 K9 Lamoge Kilken
44 D11 Lanesborough/Béal Átha Liag Roscom
26 D6 Lannaght Clare
38 F4 Laracor Meath
38 G7 Laragh Kildre
23 D2 Laragh Monhan
31 K6 Laragh/Láithreach Wicklw
5 K2 Larchill Cross Roads Cork
49 K9 Largan Mayo
22 B3 Largan Roscom
50 H10 Largan Sligo
58 E8 Largy Donegl
52 F3 Largydonnell Leitrim
63 L3 Larne Antrim
15 J8 Latnamard Monhan
25 N11 Latoon Bridge Clare
19 L8 Lattin Tippry
55 K11 Latton Monhan
3 L5 Lauragh/Láithreach Kerry
54 C4 Laurelvale Armagh
35 Q10 Laurencetown/An Baile Mór Galway
51 M10 Lavagh Sligo
56 D4 Lawrencetown Down
47 N10 Laytown/An Inse Meath
64 B10 Leabgarrow/An Leadhb Gharbh Donegl
6 D6 Leamlara Cork
4 F9 Leap/An Léim Cork
36 C4 Lecarrow Roscom
55 J2 Leckemy Donegl
33 J2 Leenaun/An Líonán Galway
36 H2 Legan or Lenamore Longfd
44 H6 Leggah Longfd
63 J8 Legoniel Antrim
24 G8 Lehinch/An Leacht Clare
22 B2 Leighlinbridge/Leithghlinn an Droichid Carlow
38 C6 Leinster Bridge Meath
17 J2 Leitrim Down
57 J6 Leitrim Down
44 C4 Leitrim/Liatroim Leitrm
17 J7 Leitrim East Kerry
4 D7 Leitry Bridge Cork
39 K7 Leixlip Kildre
36 G9 Lemanaghan Offaly
13 P8 Lemybrien/Léim Uí Bhriain Watfd
14 F8 Leperstown Watfd
16 D11 Lerrig Kerry
59 J7 Letterbarra Donegl
55 J3 Letterbreen Ferman
13 J9 Lettercallow Galway
52 F3 Letterfrack/Leitir Fraic Galway
24 H10 Letterkelly Clare
65 M11 Letterkenny/Leitir Ceanainn Donegl
67 L8 Letterloan Lderry
58 H3 Lettermacaward/Leitir Mhic an Bhaird Donegl
41 L5 Lettermaghera Mayo
33 J9 Lettermore/Leitir Móir Galway
32 H10 Lettermullan/Leitir Meallán Galway
34 H4 Levally Galway
42 B11 Levally Mayo
14 C6 Lickeystown Kilken
60 C4 Lifford/Leifear Donegl
60 E5 Ligfordrum or Douglas Tyrone
66 H9 Limavady Lderry
18 F4 Limerick/Luimneach Limrck
19 M8 Limerick Junction Tippry
65 Q6 Linsfort Donegl
35 M11 Lisbane Down
54 C5 Lisbellaw Ferman
54 G11 Lisboduff Cavan
62 H11 Lisburn Antrim
24 G8 Liscannor Galway
24 G8 Liscannor/Lios Ceannúir Clare
41 L9 Liscarney Mayo
11 L3 Liscarroll/Lios Cearúill Cork
17 M2 Liscasey Clare
38 C2 Lischerher Cross Roads Meath
60 F3 Liscloon Tyrone
8 G5 Lisdargan Kerry
24 H6 Lisdoonvarna/Lios Dúin Bhearna Clare
28 H11 Lisdowney Kilken
46 B8 Lisduff Cavan
11 Q3 Lisduff Cork
28 C3 Lisduff Offaly
44 F10 Lisduff Cross Roads Longfd
27 M9 Lisgarode Tippry
5 Q5 Lisgoold Cork
45 Q6 Lisgrea Cross Roads Cavan
17 N2 Lisheen Clare
55 P11 Lisheenaguile Galway
43 M5 Liskeagh Sligo
45 L10 Lismacaffry Wmeath
11 J4 Lismire Cork
12 H9 Lismore/Lios Mór Watfd
35 P6 Lismoyle Roscom
18 H4 Lisnadill Armagh
14 C7 Lisnagry Limrck
61 N4 Lisnakill Cross Watfd
53 P2 Lisnarrick Ferman
54 D7 Lisnaskea Ferman
5 P8 Lisnatunny Cork
8 G5 Lispatrick Cork
8 G3 Lispole/Lios Póil Kerry
25 K11 Lisroe Clare
20 F10 Lisronagh Tippry
45 K9 Lisryan Longfd

10 G11 Lissacresig Cork
43 M9 Lissalway Roscom
3 Q12 Lissamona Cork
35 O11 Lissanacody Galway
43 L8 Lissananny Roscom
5 L6 Lissaphooca Cross Roads Cork
9 J10 Lissatinnig Bridge Kerry
4 H9 Lissavard Cork
16 F8 Lisselton Cross Roads Kerry
9 N2 Listellick Kerry
21 P10 Listerlin Kilken
57 L3 Listooder Down
12 G10 Listowel/Lios Tuathail Kerry
19 L10 Lisvarrinane Tippry
6 C7 Little Island Cork
20 E5 Littleton/An Baile Beag Tippry
16 E10 Lixnaw/Leic Snámha Kerry
62 G7 Loanends Antrim
46 G8 Lobinstown Meath
45 K6 Loch Gowna/Loch Gamhna Cavan
17 L6 Loghill Limrck
14 H8 Logleagh Watfd
3 J3 Lomanagh Kerry
11 L6 Londonderry Cork
66 C11 Londonderry/Derry Lderry
28 C5 Longford Offaly
18 G2 Longford/An Longfort Longfd
18 G2 Longford Bridge Limrck
20 F3 Longfordpass Bridge Tippry
47 M8 Longwood Meath
27 M5 Lorrha/Lothra Tippry
22 C4 Lorum Carlow
7 N4 Loskeran Watfd
34 G5 Loughacutteen Tippry
22 H4 Loughacutteen Tippry
37 K5 Loughanavally Wmeath
64 E10 Loughanure Donegl
33 N10 Loughaunbeg Galway
34 G5 Loughbrickland Down
45 L6 Loughduff Cavan
9 J4 Lougher Kerry
33 M5 Loughgall Armagh
43 K7 Loughglinn/Loch Glinne Roscom
68 B8 Loughguile Antrim
57 L4 Loughinisland Down
60 H8 Loughmacrory Tyrone
20 D2 Loughmore Tippry
55 M11 Loughmorne Monhan
26 F2 Loughrea/Baile Locha Riach Galway
39 Q3 Loughshinny Dublin
40 H8 Louisburgh/Cluain Cearbán Mayo
47 J4 Louth/Lú Louth
62 E10 Lower Ballinderry Antrim
3 N10 Lowertown Cork
55 H5 Lowtown Down
51 K7 Lucan Dublin
51 K7 Lugdoon Sligo
28 E3 Luggacurren Laois
21 N10 Lukeswell Kilken
38 D9 Lullymore Kildre
42 G5 Lurga Mayo
56 D2 Lurgan Armagh
35 G2 Lurgan Offaly
43 N6 Lurgan Roscom
65 P7 Lurganboy Donegl
52 H5 Lurganboy Leitrm
39 P4 Lusk/Lusca Dublin
44 E11 Lyneen Bridge Longfd
16 G11 Lyracrumpane Kerry
11 N8 Lyradane Cork
6 C4 Lyre Cork
11 K7 Lyre Cork
11 O3 Lyre Kerry
12 F8 Lyrenaglogh Watfd

M

33 L5 Maam Cross/An Teach Dóite Galway
58 G4 Maas Donegl
41 N8 Mace Mayo
53 Q7 Mackan Ferman
12 E8 Macosquin Lderry
10 H11 Macroom/Maigh Chromtha Cork
46 B3 Madabawn Cavan
24 M5 Maddockstown Kilken
29 P9 Maganey Kildre
62 F11 Magheraberry Antrim
57 K7 Maghera Down
52 P10 Maghera Cross Roads Clare
65 N4 Magheradrumman Donegl
61 P5 Magherafelt Lderry
56 E2 Magheralin Down
66 B11 Magheramason Tyrone
63 L4 Magheramorne Antrim
54 F8 Magheraveely Ferman
17 P9 Mahoonagh Limrck
9 Q2 Maine Bridge Cork
38 G8 Mainham Kildre
39 P5 Malahide/Mullach Íde Dublin
66 D3 Malin/Málainn Donegl
58 A7 Malin Beg/Málainn Bhig Donegl
58 B7 Malin More Donegl
40 H5 Mallaranny/An Mhala Raithní Mayo
11 N6 Mallow/Mala Cork
62 H7 Mallusk Antrim
4 G6 Manch Bridge Cork
36 E8 Mannion's Cross Roads Galway
65 N10 Manorcunningham/Mainear Uí Chuinneagáin Donegl
52 H6 Manorhamilton/Cluainín Leitrm
20 E3 Manselstown Tippry
47 K5 Mansfieldstown Louth
42 B7 Mantua Roscom
20 F6 Mardyke Tippry

56 B6 Markethill Armagh
13 L4 Marifield Tippry
22 H6 Marshalstown Wexfd
18 H10 Martinstown Antrim
46 F11 Martinstown Cross Roads Meath
46 E10 Marty Meath
2 G2 Mastergeehy Kerry
20 B9 Masterstown Tippry
11 N10 Matehy Cork
4 E9 Maulatrahane Cork
4 C5 Maulawaddra Cork
3 N10 Maulawaddra Cork
33 L4 Maum Galway
33 L4 Maumtrasna Mayo
25 K9 Mauricesmills Clare
15 N6 Mayglass Wexfd
47 J7 Maynooth/Maigh Nuad Kildre
42 C9 Mayo Mayo
58 F2 Mayobridge Down
62 C11 Mazetown Antrim
67 N11 McGregor's Corner Antrim
67 N11 McLaughlins Corner Antrim
27 M3 Meanus Limrck
10 G3 Meelick Galway
64 F7 Meelin Cork
64 F7 Meenaclady/Mín an Chladaigh Donegl
58 G2 Meenacross Donegl
58 G2 Meenacross Donegl
64 D10 Meenaneary Donegl
64 F7 Meenbannad Donegl
58 C11 Meenbanivane Kerry
64 F7 Meenlaragh/Mín Lárach Donegl
2 E2 Meenanareeny Cork
31 L9 Meeting of the Waters Wicklw
26 D9 Meigh Armagh
34 C9 Menlough Armagh
33 K6 Menlough/Mionlach Galway
35 K6 Middletown Armagh
42 E6 Midfield Mayo
6 E7 Midleton/Mainistir an Corann Cork
22 H7 Milehouse Wexfd
30 E4 Milemill Kildre
19 N4 Milestone Tippry
53 P5 Milford Donegl
18 C11 Milford/Áth an Mhuilinn Cork
62 E6 Mill Town Antrim
63 K3 Millbrook Antrim
4 E9 Milleen Bridge Cork
57 M8 Milford/Baile na nGallóglach Donegl
63 P8 Millisle Down
52 E7 Millstreet Cork
13 L8 Millstreet Watfd
10 G7 Millstreet/Sráid an Mhuilinn Cork
56 B4 Milltown Armagh
54 C11 Milltown Cavan
58 H8 Milltown Donegl
65 M6 Milltown Donegl
39 S3 Milltown Dublin
35 L4 Milltown Galway
14 C3 Milltown Kilken
64 F7 Milltown Lderry
67 M9 Milltown Lderry
37 K4 Milltown Wmeath
8 E5 Milltown/Baile an Mhuilinn Cork
9 N5 Milltown/Baile an Mhuilinn Kerry
18 E11 Milltown Cross Roads Cork
24 G10 Milltown Malbay/Sráid na Cathrach Clare
37 P6 Milltownpass/Bealach Bhaile an Mhuileann Wmeath
57 M6 Minane Bridge Cork
13 N4 Minorstown Tippry
12 D6 Mitchelstown/Baile Mhisteala Cork
16 G4 Moanmore Clare
19 K9 Moanmore Tippry
44 H9 Moat Farrell Longfd
36 G7 Moate/An Móta Wmeath
11 L10 Model Village Cork
11 N11 Model Village Cork
13 L9 Modelligo Watfd
16 A3 Modreeny Tippry
6 G6 Mogeely Cork
21 M3 Mohil Kilken
44 E5 Mohill/Maothail Leitrm
62 E11 Moira Down
9 P10 Moll's Gap Kerry
22 H4 Monagear Wexfd
55 K7 Monaghan/Muineachán Monhan
55 K7 Monaghan County Museum Monhan
6 F3 Monaloun Watfd
13 J8 Monalour Watfd
46 H9 Monamintra Cross Roads Watfd
23 L6 Monamolin Wexfd
7 M4 Monamraher Watfd
19 L7 Monard Tippry
23 K3 Moneard Wexfd
48 E7 Monaster Limrck
43 L5 Monasteraden Sligo
21 K7 Monasterboice Louth
29 M3 Monasterevin/Mainistir Eimhín Kildre
11 N7 Monea Tippry
44 C11 Monea Cross Roads Fermn
11 N7 Moneen Cork
23 K3 Moneen Galway
29 L10 Moneenroe Kilken
28 G2 Monettia Bog Laois
64 G9 Money More Donegl
4 H3 Moneycusker Cork
67 P9 Moneygall/Muine Gall Offaly
53 M7 Moneygashel Cavan
53 Q5 Moneyglass Antrim
64 E7 Moneymore Lderry
61 M4 Moneyneany Lderry
63 L10 Moneyreagh Down
56 N3 Moneyslane Down
37 N3 Monilea Wmeath

34 H7 Monivea/Muine Mheá Galway
63 J6 Monkstown Antrim
6 C8 Monkstown Cork
18 H2 Montpelier Limrck
14 C5 Mooncoin/Móin Choinn Kilken
30 C7 Moone/Maoin Kildre
7 K6 Moord Watfd
27 L2 Moorfield Cross Roads Galway
62 F4 Moorfields Antrim
11 O3 Moran's Cross Roads Lderry
18 D8 Morenane Limrck
10 B10 Morley's Bridge Kerry
47 M9 Mornington Meath
19 N7 Morpeth Bridge Tippry
45 N11 Mortlestown Limrck
5 L4 Moskeagh Cork
47 N11 Mosney Camp Meath
55 J7 Mossley Antrim
67 Q6 Moss-Side Antrim
21 Q5 Mottel Watfd
45 N7 Mount Nugent Cavan
63 P10 Mount Stewart Down
55 P4 Mount Talbot Roscom
52 D3 Mount Temple Sligo
36 G6 Mount Temple Wmeath
6 C8 Mount Uniacke Cork
47 N3 Mountain Bay Louth
53 J11 Mountain Roscom
35 L5 Mountbellew Bridge/An Creagán Galway
23 D2 Mountbolus Offaly
6 C4 Mountcatherine Cork
64 J8 Mountcharles/Móin Séarlas Donegl
10 E2 Mountcollins Limrck
60 G8 Mountfield Tyrone
23 L6 Mounthoward Cross Roads Wexfd
60 E8 Mountjoy Tyrone
13 J8 Mountmelleray Watfd
29 J4 Mountmellick/Móinteach Míllic Laois
56 B7 Mountnorris Armagh
28 G7 Mountrath/Maighean Rátha Laois
16 G2 Mountrivers Bridge Clare
26 M8 Mountshannon/Baile Uí Bheoláin Clare
56 H10 Mourne Park Down
16 E4 Moveen Clare
66 G6 Moville/Bun an Phobail Donegl
25 N4 Moy Galway
55 N2 Moy Tyrone
19 L2 Moyard Galway
42 G5 Moyasta Clare
20 D5 Moycarky Tippry
34 B8 Moycullen/Maigh Cuilinn Galway
44 F11 Moydow Longfd
61 N11 Moygashel Tyrone
20 E7 Moyglass Tippry
30 C11 Moyle Carlow
43 K5 Moylisha Wicklw
26 C10 Moylough Sligo
43 J9 Moymore Clare
25 J4 Moynalty/Maigh nEalta Meath
38 G5 Moyvalvy Meath
44 H5 Moyne Roscom
20 E3 Moyne Roscom
30 H9 Moyne Wicklw
4 D7 Moyny Bridge Cork
48 F7 Moyrahan Mayo
19 M7 Moyrus Limrck
32 G7 Moyus Carlow
66 H10 Moys Down
38 D6 Moyvore Wmeath
54 H4 Moyvore Wmeath
36 H6 Moyvoughly Wmeath
38 E7 Muckloon Kildre
38 E7 Muckross Kerry
9 R8 Muckross House Kerry
10 B2 Muff/Magh Donegl
9 L7 Muinganear Kerry
9 Q2 Muingaphuca Kerry
16 H11 Muingnaminnane Kerry
2 E2 Muinydowda Kerry
39 L6 Mulhuddart Dublin
50 D8 Mulafarry Mayo
24 F11 Mulagh Clare
35 M11 Mullagh Galway
41 J9 Mullagh Mayo
35 J8 Mullagh Meath
44 C7 Mullaghanish Cavan
56 B10 Mullaghbane Armagh
52 E2 Mullaghmore Sligo
43 L4 Mullaghroe Sligo
67 L9 Mullan Lderry
67 P10 Mullan Head Antrim
51 J11 Mullany's Cross Sligo
47 H9 Mullany Cross Roads Louth
21 Q7 Mullen Roscom
11 Q7 Mullenaboree Cork
21 J9 Mullennaglogh Tippry
21 P9 Mullennakill Kilken
30 G11 Mullinavat Wicklw
20 H7 Mullinahone/Muileann na hUamhan Tippry
14 D4 Mullinavat/Muileann an Bhata Kilken
37 M4 Mullingar/An Muileann gCearr Wmeath
42 B10 Mullingar Bridge Mayo
22 D11 Multyfarnham/Muilte Farannáin Wmeath
18 E5 Mungret/Mungairit Limrck
17 J8 Murher Kerry
6 G4 Murley's Cross Roads Cork
15 N5 Murrisk Kerry
30 D4 Murragh/An Mhulríoch Kerry
41 K8 Murrisk Mayo
19 J4 Murroe Cork
14 H4 Murroogh Clare
40 E4 Mweelin Kerry
9 R3 Mweenalaaa Kerry
4 G5 Myross Cork
6 C10 Myrtleville Cork
22 E3 Myshall/Míseal Carlow

2 F2 **Sallahig** Kerry
38 G10 **Sallins**/*Na Solláin* Kildre
6 B6 **Sallybrook** Cork
27 N11 **Sallypark** Tippry
34 C10 **Saltmill**/*Bóthar na Trá* Galway
14 H7 **Saltmills** Wexfd
61 M9 **Sandholes** Tyrone
39 N9 **Sandyford** Dublin
39 N9 **Santry** Dublin
21 K3 **Sart Cross Roads** Kilken
57 N4 **Saul** Down
10 D3 **Scalp Bridge** Kerry
35 Q3 **Scardaun** Roscom
42 D11 **Scardaune** Mayo
23 N2 **Scarnagh Cross Roads** Wexfd
38 D4 **Scarriff Bridge** Meath
26 F9 **Scarriff**/*An Scairbh* Clare
13 M8 **Scart Bridge** Watfd
10 B5 **Scartaglin**/*Scairteach an Chlinne* Kerry
56 D5 **Scarva** Down
56 D5 **Scotch Corner** Monhan
56 B2 **Scotch Street** Armagh
54 F10 **Scotshouse** Monhan
55 J6 **Scotstown**/*Baile an Scotaigh* Monhan
10 C6 **Scrahanfadda** Kerry
44 C9 **Scramoge** Roscom
12 B8 **Scrarour** Cork
23 K9 **Screen** Wexfd
37 H10 **Screggan** Offaly
66 H11 **Scriggan** Lderry
46 D10 **Scurlockstown** Meath
57 L5 **Seaforde** Down
13 N4 **Seapatrick** Down
13 N4 **Seskin** Tippry
60 F11 **Seskinore** Tyrone
4 E5 **Shanacrane** Cork
6 G8 **Shanagarry** Cork
25 P6 **Shanaglish** Galway
17 N6 **Shanagolden**/*Seanghualainn* Limrck
28 G8 **Shanahoe** Laois
24 H10 **Shanavogh East** Clare
35 K8 **Shanballard** Galway
6 C9 **Shanbally** Cork
35 L2 **Shanbally** Galway
15 P9 **Shanbally** Watfd
19 L4 **Shanballyedmond** Tippry
42 G11 **Shanballymore** Galway
11 Q4 **Shanbally**/*An Seanbhaile Mór* Cork
38 D4 **Shancarrig Bridge** Meath
26 H3 **Shangarry** Galway
35 Q10 **Shankill** Dublin
4 Q5 **Shanlaragh** Cork
46 H7 **Shanlis Cross Roads** Louth
17 M5 **Shannakea** Clare
18 B3 **Shannon** Clare
36 D11 **Shannon Harbour**/*Caladh na Sionainne* Offaly
36 C9 **Shannonbridge**/*Droichead na Sionainne* Offaly
29 M8 **Shanragh** Laois
12 G6 **Shanrahan Cross Roads** Tippry
17 P10 **Shanrath** Limrck
40 D2 **Shantonagh** Monhan
27 Q6 **Sharavogue** Offaly
44 D3 **Shercock**/*Searcóg* Cavan
04 Q4 **Sheskin** Watfd
19 P4 **Shevry** Tippry
12 H2 **Shillelagh**/*Síol Ealaigh* Wicklw
27 Q7 **Shinrone**/*Suí an Róin* Offaly
57 N3 **Shrigley** Down
19 L8 **Shronell** Tippry
16 G7 **Shronew** Kerry
34 C4 **Shrule**/*Sruthair* Mayo
4 E6 **Silahertane** Cork
58 B10 **Silver Bridge** Armagh
55 L6 **Silver Stream** Monhan
27 K11 **Silvermines**/*Béal Átha Gabhann* Tippry
60 C5 **Sion Mills** Tyrone
63 N8 **Six Road Ends** Down
18 D2 **Sixmilebridge**/*Droichead Abhainn Ó gCearnaigh* Clare
60 H10 **Sixmilecross** Tyrone
4 B6 **Skahanagh** Cork
6 C5 **Skahanagh North** Cork
6 C5 **Skahanagh South** Cork
4 C9 **Skeagh** Cork
37 J4 **Skeagh Beg** Wmeath
26 C4 **Skehanagh** Galway
36 J6 **Skehanagh** Galway
12 E6 **Skeheen** Cork
11 P5 **Skenakilla Cross Roads** Cork
39 Q2 **Skerries**/*Na Sceirí* Dublin
4 D10 **Skibbereen**/*An Sciobairín* Cork
39 J2 **Screen** Meath
51 L7 **Screen** Sligo
3 P10 **Skull**/*An Scoil* Cork
53 L8 **Slade** Watfd
47 J10 **Slane**/*Baile Shláine* Meath
35 M3 **Slievemurray** Galway
14 E6 **Slieveowen** Cork
14 E6 **Slieverue** Kilken
52 D6 **Sligga Bridge** Cork
52 D6 **Sligo**/*Sligeach* Sligo
52 D6 **Sligo Abbey** Sligo
47 J7 **Smarmore** Louth
6 C4 **Smerwick** Kerry
54 H7 **Smithborough** Monhan
29 L11 **Smithstown** Kilken
3 J3 **Sneem**/*An tSnaidhm* Kerry
52 E9 **Sooey** Sligo
9 M2 **Spa** Kerry
25 N9 **Spancehill** Cork
24 F10 **Spanish Point**/*Rinn na Spáinneach* Clare
61 J5 **Sperrin** Tyrone
33 P10 **Spiddle**/*An Spidéal* Galway
25 K9 **Spink Bridge** Laois
37 J7 **Spittaltown** Wmeath
66 C10 **Spring Town** Lderry
31 L4 **Srah** Mayo
48 P10 **Srah**/*An tSraith* Mayo
42 C6 **Srahanboy** Laois
42 C6 **Sraheens** Mayo
48 H9 **Sraheens Bridge** Mayo
48 H11 **Srahnamanragh Bridge** Mayo

49 K5 **Sranataggle** Mayo
13 J8 **Sruh** Watfd
47 K6 **Stabannan** Louth
46 H10 **Stackallan** Meath
72 C6 **Staffordstown** Antrim
47 N11 **Stamullin** Meath
38 F8 **Stapletown** Kildre
39 N10 **Stepaside** Dublin
61 P9 **Stewartstown** Tyrone
39 N9 **Stillorgan** Dublin
54 G8 **Stone Bridge** Monhan
48 H5 **Stonefield** Mayo
6 G8 **Stonepark** Limrck
62 G9 **Stonyford** Antrim
21 M7 **Stonyford**/*Áth Stúin* Kilken
63 L9 **Stormont** Down
60 C4 **Strabane** Tyrone
8 H3 **Stradbally** Kerry
29 L6 **Stradbally**/*An tSráidbhaile* Laois
13 Q9 **Stradbally**/*An tSráidbhaile* Watfd
42 C5 **Strade** Mayo
45 P4 **Stradone**/*Sraith an Domhain*
38 H9 **Straffan**/*Teach Srafáin* Kildre
14 H7 **Strahart** Wexfd
63 J5 **Straid** Antrim
17 M10 **Strand** Limrck
51 N6 **Strandhill**/*An Leathros* Sligo
57 P4 **Strangford** Down
67 P2 **Strancum** Antrim
59 P4 **Stranorlar**/*Srath an Urláir* Donegl
30 E7 **Stratford**/*Áth na Sráide* Wicklw
37 J6 **Streamstown** Wmeath
45 K10 **Street** Wmeath
28 C11 **Strogue Cross Roads** Tippry
44 B8 **Strokestown**/*Béal na mBuillí* Roscom
44 B8 **Strokestown Park** Roscom
26 H5 **Stroove** Donegl
11 L9 **Stuake** Cork
5 Q7 **Summer Cove** Cork
38 F5 **Summerhill**/*Cnoc an Linsigh* Meath
30 C4 **Suncroft** Kildre
29 L9 **Swan** Laois
55 J9 **Swan's Cross Roads** Monhan
53 P8 **Swanlinbar**/*An Muileann Iarainn* Cavan
P1 P2 **Swatragh** Lderry
42 E5 **Swinford**/*Béal Átha na Muice* Mayo
39 N5 **Swords**/*Sord* Dublin

T

35 Q7 **Taghmaconnell** Roscom
15 L5 **Taghmon**/*Teach Munna* Wexfd
36 H2 **Taghshinny** Longfd
15 Q6 **Tagoat** Wexfd
3 K5 **Tahilla** Kerry
38 L9 **Tallaght** Dublin
47 J5 **Tallanstown** Louth
12 G10 **Tallow**/*Tulach an Iarainn* Watfd
12 H10 **Tallowbridge** Watfd
54 B5 **Tamlaht** Ferman
61 Q2 **Tamlaght O'Crilly** Lderry
61 P11 **Tamnamore** Tyrone
56 C4 **Tandragee** Armagh
36 F4 **Tang** Wmeath
18 F10 **Tankardstown** Limrck
13 K6 **Tar Bridge** Tippry
38 H5 **Tara** Meath
37 J8 **Tara** Meath
17 J4 **Tarbert**/*Tairbeart* Kerry
17 J4 **Tarmon** Clare
11 K2 **Tarrant's Cross Roads** Cork
55 P6 **Tassagh** Armagh
10 F4 **Taur** Cork
65 M4 **Tawny** Donegl
42 G5 **Tawnyinah** Mayo
45 N4 **Tawnylea** Leitrm
27 P3 **Taylor's Cross** Offaly
3 Q7 **Tedagh** Cork
15 J6 **Tedavnet** Monhan
58 C8 **Teelin**/*Tíeleann* Donegl
54 C9 **Teemore** Ferman
8 G3 **Teer** Kerry
2 D2 **Teeranearagh** Kerry
8 G3 **Teernahillane** Cork
4 B7 **Teeretton** Cork
25 M11 **Teermaclane** Clare
33 L4 **Teernakill Bridge** Galway
8 H9 **Teeromoyle** Kerry
46 D6 **Teevurcher** Meath
51 K7 **Templeboy** Sligo
19 N2 **Templederry** Tippry
13 N3 **Templetney** Tippry
28 B11 **Templemore**/*An Teampall Mór* Tippry
15 M8 **Templenoe** Kerry
37 M7 **Templeoran** Wmeath
14 B3 **Templeorum** Kilken
62 G6 **Templepatrick** Antrim
22 F6 **Templeshanbo** Wexfd
28 C11 **Templetouhy**/*Teampall Tuaithe* Tippry
14 H8 **Templetown** Wexfd
6 B6 **Templeusque** Cork
54 D4 **Tempo** Ferman
13 N5 **Tenacre Cross Roads** Wexfd
47 M8 **Termon**
48 E9 **Termonbarry** Roscom
47 M8 **Termonfeckin**/*Tearmann Feichín* Louth
27 L5 **Terryglass**/*Tír Dhá Ghlas* Tippry
37 P3 **Tevrin** Wmeath
36 J8 **The Battery** Tippry
47 N3 **The Bush** Louth
21 P2 **The Butts** Carlow
66 D11 **The Cross** Lderry
61 G8 **The Diamond** Antrim
67 P4 **The Diamond** Tyrone
61 G8 **The Downs** Wmeath
58 B8 **The Drones** Antrim
39 N3 **The Five Roads** Dublin
24 H10 **The Hand Cross Roads** Clare
23 K6 **The Harrow** Wexfd

22 F10 **The Leap** Wexfd
61 Q7 **The Loup** Lderry
36 F4 **The Pigeons** Wmeath
27 N6 **The Pike** Tippry
6 H4 **The Pike** Watfd
15 P9 **The Pike** Watfd
61 M9 **The Rock** Tyrone
22 C9 **The Rower** Kilken
62 G2 **The Sheddings** Antrim
61 L5 **The Six Towns** Lderry
57 K4 **The Spa** Down
14 B4 **The Sweep** Kilken
63 K11 **The Temple** Down
18 H11 **Thomastown** Limrck
46 E8 **Thomastown** Meath
19 P8 **Thomastown** Tippry
21 N7 **Thomastown**/*Baile Mhic Andáin* Kilken
55 J7 **Three Mile House** Monhan
21 L3 **Threecastles** Kilken
31 K9 **Threewells** Wicklw
20 H3 **Thurles**/*Durlas* Tippry
43 L6 **Tibohine** Roscom
16 A9 **Tiduff** Kerry
13 M4 **Tikincor** Watfd
58 E8 **Timahoe** Kildre
29 K7 **Timahoe**/*Tigh Mochua* Laois
5 L8 **Timoleague**/*Tigh Molaige* Cork
30 D7 **Timolin** Kildre
30 H11 **Timahely**/*Tigh na hÉilie* Wicklw
56 G8 **Tinamuck** Offaly
23 J7 **Tinnacross Cross Roads** Kilken
22 H10 **Tinnakilla** Wexfd
29 P11 **Tinryland** Carlow
47 K8 **Tinure Cross Roads** Louth
19 M8 **Tipperary**/*Tiobraid Árann* Tippry
61 N3 **Tirkane** Lderry
55 K6 **Tirnanean** Cork
55 P5 **Tirnaneill** Monhan
53 K8 **Tirnevin** Galway
34 H7 **Tober** Cavan
62 H2 **Tobercurry**/*Tobar an Choire* Sligo
26 D3 **Toberelatan** Galway
61 N4 **Tobermore** Lderry
10 H3 **Tobermacdougha Cross Roads** Cork
34 C3 **Tobernadarry** Mayo
52 D9 **Toberscanavan** Sligo
4 F5 **Toem** Tippry
47 M7 **Togher** Louth
38 E5 **Togher** Meath
37 P8 **Togher** Meath
30 H5 **Togher** Wicklw
16 C10 **Togherbane** Kerry
15 N7 **Tomhaggard** Wexfd
52 A5 **Tonabrocky** Galway
40 G4 **Tonregee** Mayo
86 B4 **Tonyduff** Cavan
4 G5 **Toom** Cork
25 J5 **Toomaghera** Clare
41 P11 **Toomakeady**/*Tuar Mhic Éadaigh* Mayo
35 L4 **Toomard** Galway
32 G6 **Toombeola** Galway
62 B5 **Toome** Antrim
4 H3 **Tooms** Cork
27 N10 **Toomyvara**/*Tuaim Uí Mheára* Tippry
19 L3 **Toor** Tippry
13 L7 **Tooraneena** Watfd
11 Q7 **Tooraree** Limrck
19 L3 **Tooreenbrien Bridge** Tippry
10 D5 **Tooreencahill** Kerry
10 G3 **Tooreendermot** Cork
22 C9 **Toorgarriff** Cork
5 N10 **Toormore** Cork
11 M11 **Toornafulla** Limrck
37 L7 **Torque** Wmeath
66 C10 **Tower Museum** Lderry
6 D9 **Towergare** Watfd
6 B10 **Tracton** Cork
3 M7 **Trafrask** Cork
9 N3 **Tralee**/*Trá Lí* Kerry
14 D3 **Tramore**/*Trá Mhór* Watfd
35 J4 **Trasternagh** Galway
2 H7 **Travara Bridge** Cork
4 B7 **Trawlebane** Cork
33 N2 **Trean** Mayo
65 L10 **Treantagh** Donegl
53 P11 **Treehoo Cross Roads** Cavan
9 J3 **Treech Bridge** Kerry
43 K9 **Trien** Roscom
54 C2 **Trillick** Tyrone
38 F3 **Trim**/*Baile Átha Troim* Meath
38 F3 **Trim Castle** Meath
35 M8 **Trust** Galway
34 F4 **Tuam**/*Tuaim* Watfd
26 F9 **Tuamgraney**/*Tuaim Gréine* Clare
25 P7 **Tubber** Galway
20 H3 **Tubbrid** Kilken
12 H5 **Tubbrid** Tippry
12 H5 **Tuar**/*An Tulach* Clare
4 E4 **Tullagh** Cork
25 J11 **Tullaghaboy** Clare
52 F2 **Tullaghan** Leitrm
48 G10 **Tullaghan**
21 P9 **Tullagher** Kilken
21 K9 **Tullaghought** Kilken
21 N6 **Tullakeel** Kerry
3 J2 **Tullamaine** Kilken
37 K9 **Tullamore**/*Tulach Mhór* Offaly
9 J3 **Tullaree** Kerry
21 J4 **Tullaroan** Kilken
25 L10 **Tullassa** Clare
16 C5 **Tullig** Kerry
16 G10 **Tullig** Kerry
30 E11 **Tullow**/*An Tulach* Carlow
33 M10 **Tully**/*An Tulaigh* Galway
32 F2 **Tully Cross** Galway
47 K9 **Tullyallen** Louth
15 L6 **Tullycanna** Wexfd
52 G8 **Tullycoly** Leitrm

61 N9 **Tullyhogue** Tyrone
11 J2 **Tullylease** Cork
42 Q2 **Tullyvin** Cavan
42 G10 **Tulrohaun** Mayo
43 P8 **Tulsk**/*Tuilsce* Roscom
37 P3 **Tuosist** Kerry
25 L4 **Turlough** Clare
42 B6 **Turlough** Mayo
29 F2 **Turloughmore** Galway
4 E5 **Turnapidogy** Cork
11 P4 **Turnpike Cross** Cork
44 D11 **Turreen** Longfd
11 P6 **Tweelacare Cross Roads** Wexfd
20 C5 **Tworford Bridges** Tippry
28 H3 **Twomile Bridge** Laois
20 E4 **Twomileborris** Tippry
23 J3 **Tynagh** Galway
55 M5 **Tynan** Armagh
61 N11 **Tyrone Crystal** Tyrone
37 M7 **Tyrrellspass**/*Bealach an Tirialaigh* Wmeath

U

60 E8 **Ulster American Folk Park** Tyrone
4 F10 **Unionhall**/*Bréantrá* Cork
62 F10 **Upper Ballinderry** Antrim
19 P3 **Upperchurch** Tippry
P3 P3 **Upperlands** Lderry
5 M5 **Upton** Cork
2 H7 **Urhin** Cork
42 H7 **Urlaur** Mayo
20 G3 **Urlingford**/*Áth na nÚrlainn* Kilken

V

30 G4 **Valleymount** Wicklw
8 D5 **Ventry** Kerry
39 J2 **Vicarstown** Laois
60 D5 **Victoria Bridge** Tyrone
13 K10 **Villierstown**/*An Baile Nua* Watfd
46 B7 **Virginia**/*Achadh an Iúir* Cavan

W

37 P10 **Walsh Island** Offaly
4 E5 **Walshtown** Cork
39 J2 **Walterstown** Wmeath
38 H5 **Ward** Dublin
39 N9 **Waringstown** Down
56 E2 **Warner's Cross Roads** Cork
5 P4 **Warrenpoint** Down
56 E10 **Watch House Cross Roads** Kildre
22 G3 **Watch House Village** Wexfd
5 P3 **Waterfall** Cork
14 E8 **Waterford**/*Port Láirge* Watfd
14 E8 **Waterford** Watfd
14 D6 **Waterford Crystal** Watfd
6 C5 **Watergrasshill**/*Cnocán na Biolraí* Cork
2 F3 **Waterville**/*An Coireán* Kerry
59 N4 **Welchtown** Donegl
15 K6 **Wellingtonbridge**/*Droichead Eoin* Wexfd
5 J8 **West Cork Model Railway Village** Cork
64 F4 **West Town**/*Baile Thiar* Donegl
41 M8 **Westport**/*Cathair na Mart* Mayo
41 L8 **Westport Quay** Mayo
14 D9 **Westtown** Watfd
39 N9 **Wexford**/*Loch Garman* Wexfd
30 C2 **Wheelann Cross Roads** Kildre
11 Q10 **White's Cross** Cork
9 M5 **White Gate Cross Roads** Cork
63 K7 **Whiteabbey** Antrim
11 L9 **Whitechurch** Cork
11 L9 **Whitechurch** Watfd
15 K9 **Whitechurch** Wexfd
56 B7 **Whitecross** Armagh
26 H8 **Whitegate**/*An Geata Bán* Clare
6 D9 **Whitegate**/*An Geata Bán* Cork
44 E9 **Whitehall** Roscom
45 N11 **Whitehall** Wmeath
47 P3 **Whites Town** Louth
62 D4 **Whitesides Corner** Antrim
31 P7 **Wicklow**/*Cill Mhantáin* Wicklw
46 G9 **Wilkinstown**/*Baile Uilcín* Meath
25 K8 **Willbrook** Clare
43 K11 **Williamstown** Galway
21 K9 **Windgap**/*Bearna na Gaoithe* Kilken
38 D8 **Windmill Cross Roads** Kildre
12 L9 **Wolfhill** Laois
15 K9 **Woodburn** Antrim
31 L10 **Woodenbridge** Wicklw
26 D11 **Woodfield Bridge** Clare
26 H5 **Woodford**/*An Chraig* Galway
35 L8 **Woodlawn**/*Móta* Galway
14 F7 **Woodstown** Watfd

Y

46 H10 **Yellow Furze** Meath
27 J9 **Youghal** Tippry
3 K6 **Youghal**/*Eochaill* Cork